A must read . . . positive and profound! Rabbi Baruch HaLevi, a survivor of the dark night of the soul, brilliantly weaves together life-saving strands of ancient and modern insight that helpfully guide the reader from the darkness of despair to the light of life ... This book is for anyone searching for wholeness within the depths of a broken heart.

Marvin R. Wilson, Professor of Biblical and Theological Studies, Gordon College and author of *Our Father Abraham: Jewish Roots of the Christian Faith*

Inspirational and illuminating... We all need support and guidance through the journey of life and death. Rabbi B lifts the spirit and guides the soul for anyone navigating through the darkness of grief. Essential reading for anyone seeking to integrate spiritual insights as they journey from darkness to light.

Rebecca Rosen, world renowned spiritual medium and author of best selling books, *Spirited* and *Awaken the Spirit Within* - and Rabbi B's sister too!

An invaluable companion... This book is an invaluable companion for anyone navigating through darkness in search of light. With candor and wisdom, Rabbi HaLevi draws sparks of light even from the suicides and suffering his family endured, to guide us toward openness, acceptance and insight.

Rabbi Elie Spitz, author of *Healing from Despair: Choosing Wholeness in a Broken World*

SPARK SEEKERS

* * *

MOURNING WITH MEANING; LIVING WITH LIGHT

www.sparkseekersthebook.com

ISBN-13: 9780692404164 (Galil Mountain Media)
ISBN-10: 0692404163
Library of Congress Control Number: 2015904114
Galil Mountain Media Boston, MA

DEDICATION:

This book is dedicated to my mother, a woman who taught me through example what it means to be a spark seeker, and to my father, a man whose fire I carry with me to illuminate my path.

Rob,

It is a privilege
& honor to be
building not simply a
company w- you -
but a brotherhood &
source of healing en
the world.   your brother
                        B

CONTENTS

Introduction: The Parable of the Mustard Seed ix

Chapter 1: Darkness Descends 1

Chapter 2: Demons in the Dark 13

Chapter 3: The Void Dance 31

Chapter 4: Right into the Dark 45

Chapter 5: Rites within the Dark 63

Chapter 6: The Dark Night of the Soul 73

Chapter 7: Breaking Dawn 87

Chapter 8: Spark Seekers 99

Chapter 9: Illuminating the Path 113

Chapter 10: Carrying the Fire 129

Conclusion: The Light of Day 145

Acknowledgments 151

About the Authors 153

Notes 155

THE PARABLE OF THE MUSTARD SEED

K isa grew up in India a long time ago. She married and went to live with her husband's family, and when her son was born, all traces of homesickness vanished. Her son became ill and died, and she was stricken with grief. She carried her dead son through the village, begging for medicine to restore him to life.

A wise man saw her desperate condition and told her that the Buddha was staying nearby. He suggested that she go to him for help.

She found the Buddha sitting under the shade of a tree. He looked up at her, saw how distraught she was, and asked if he could be of service.

"My name is Kisa," she said. "I have been looking everywhere for medicine for my son."

He looked at the boy in her arms. "If you want to make the medicine, you must have some mustard seeds. Go into town and ask at each house, but you must accept seeds only from a house in which no one has died."

She set off into town to get the mustard seeds. At the first house, a young woman answered the door.

"Could I have some mustard seeds to make some medicine?" Kisa asked.

The woman went inside and soon returned with some seeds. "Here you are," she said.

As Kisa was about to accept the seeds, she remembered the condition the Buddha had set upon receipt of the seeds. "Has anyone died in this house?" she asked.

The young woman sighed. "Yes, a few months ago, my grandmother died. Why do you ask?"

Kisa said sadly, "Thank you for the seeds, but I can take them only from a house in which no one has died."

She said good-bye and went on the next house. An old man was sitting outside.

"Excuse me. Do you have any extra mustard seeds I can have?"

The old man got up, went into the house, and emerged moments later with the requested seeds.

"There you go." He held out his hand.

Again, just as Kisa was about to take the seeds, she remembered what the Buddha had said. "Has anyone died in this house?" she asked.

"Yes, last year my daughter died." He shared some memories of his child.

She said, "I'm sorry for your loss. Thank you for getting me the seeds, but I'm afraid I can't take them after all."

At the next house, a young boy answered the door.

She asked, "I'm in need of some mustard seeds. Might you have any?"

The boy smiled, ran back inside, and returned with the seeds. Placing them in her hand, he said, "Here you are."

Kisa looked into his eyes and asked, "Can you tell me if anyone has ever died in this house?"

The boy said quietly, "Yes. When I was a little baby, my daddy died. My mother likes to tell me stories about him."

"I'm sorry about your father, and thank you for getting me the seeds, but I can't use them."

As Kisa went through the village, knocking on door after door, the answer was the same. Everyone had lost a loved one at some time. She had no mustard seeds to make a medicine to bring her son back to life, but now she understood. She looked at her son in her arms with great love and set out to lay him to rest.

When she returned to the Buddha under the tree, she was no longer carrying her son, and she was calmer.

The Buddha said, "Have you been able to find the mustard seeds?"

She looked into his eyes and said, "No, but now I understand that everyone loses people they love. I have laid my son to rest."

"You have learned well, Kisa," he said. "Would you like to stay with me for a while?"

As the sun went down over Kapilavattu, they talked. She told the Buddha about her life and her son while he listened. He reminded her that plants grow in the spring, flower in the summer, and die in the winter. New plants grow the following year. Similarly, people are born and eventually die. Kisa sat under the tree alongside the Buddha with the deep understanding that this was way things are.

Death's Darkness

Sooner or later, we will stand at the grave of someone we care for, hold the ashes of someone we cherish, or stare longingly out the window of a home that feels empty. You may be standing at the precipice of loss at this moment.

It's only a matter of time before the pain of death's darkness shatters our hearts. Part of living in this world entails bearing witness to this unbearable reality. To know death is to know darkness, and when the darkness descends after the loss of someone we love, it can feel as if we're suffocating in the grip of grief. Some of us get lost in the darkness and carry it with us for years, believing it's our burden to bear and allowing it to keep us frozen in grief.

For some of us, when the darkness descends, we delude ourselves into thinking that if we run faster, we will outpace it. We believe that if we stop and enter that space, we will drown in a sea of sorrow. When we go to either extreme—indefinitely wandering in the darkness or avoiding it altogether—we lose access to the thing that can bring healing, transformation, purpose, and even blessing. We lose the opportunity to discover the sparks of light buried in the darkness of grief. These sparks are waiting for us to take hold of them so that we can carry them forward as we journey from death's darkness to life's light.

As a rabbi, and having mourned the suicides of my paternal grandmother and my father, I understand the depths of despair that individuals, families, and communities experience when death claims loved ones. I understand what it means to avoid the darkness, and I have experienced the feeling of being tossed about in the spin cycle of grief. In my personal and professional experience, I have come to understand that the darkness of grief is the most complicated experience we can confront and one of the greatest teachers we will ever know. By touching our darkness, we also touch our light.

Life's Light

We don't have a choice about the darkness that descends in the wake of losing someone we love, but we do have a choice to make: whether or not we will enter the darkness, seek sparks of light, and return to life.

I have seen individuals and families crumble under the weight of death's darkness. Alternately, I have witnessed the most courageous and inspirational expressions of what human beings are capable of when facing devastation. I have watched people transform within the darkness. I have witnessed individuals choose to live with more, not less, love and joy under the burden of grief. I have watched families grow closer and communities grow stronger as they rally to support one another. I have seen survivors of loss choose to find meaning within the darkness when everything within them believed there was none.

I have seen people rise up and live with even greater awareness, intention, and passion than they did before their losses. These people have taught me that in the darkest recesses of suffering, there's light in the form of opportunities and possibilities, potential and purpose, and beauty and blessings. There are sparks waiting for us to discover and carry out of the darkness.

But, But, But...There's a Choice

But the despair is too great—we naturally react.
But the pain is too much to bear—we undoubtedly feel.
But there's nothing but devastation in the depths of the darkness— we inevitably conclude.

But the truth is that we can endure far more than we realize.
But the truth is that despair can be overcome.
But the truth is that the darkness can be dispelled.

There are seeds of possibility within the depths of despair. In the words of Helen Keller, "Although the world is full of suffering, it is also full of the overcoming of it." The question isn't whether there are sparks of meaning, possibility, and blessings within the darkness; the question is whether we're willing to seek them.

A woman who lost her adult daughter to cancer told me that she cringed when others told her, "You're strong. You'll get over the grief."

She told them, "You don't get *over* the grief, but you can go *through* it."

Dr. Alan Wolfelt, an author, educator, and grief counselor, says, "To heal in grief, one must turn inward, slow down, embrace pain, and seek and accept support."[1] When we consciously choose to enter death's darkness, we begin to dispel that darkness. When we courageously explore it, searching for a pathway through the heartache by gathering sparks of light, we begin to move through the darkness with vision. When we pick ourselves up, dust ourselves off, and reclaim the rhythms and responsibilities of our lives, we slowly begin to see. The moment we decide to become "spark seekers" is the moment that the darkness begins to recede, making way for a new dawn. Meister Eckhart, a thirteenth-century German theologian and philosopher, said, "It is in darkness that one finds the light, so when we are in sorrow, then this light is nearest of all to us."

First Steps

This isn't to say that there's one way to grieve or one timetable for mourning. On the contrary, everyone's grief journey is unique.

The first step in becoming a spark seeker is to recognize this and to give yourself permission to be wherever you need to be, to feel whatever you're feeling, and to wander into the darkness in your own time. However, it isn't a permanent dwelling place. After your senses adjust and you find the edges of your darkness, there's an opportunity to search for the sparks of possibility, potential, hope, blessings, and beauty that lie within the dark. As you cultivate those sparks, you'll find the love and light that will accompany you as you move toward living in a world without your loved one.

This Jewish folktale will guide you as you take your first steps along this path:

A group of students wanted to drive darkness from the world, and they went to their rabbi for advice.

He said, "Take a broom, and sweep the darkness from a cellar."

It did no good.

He said, "Take sticks, and beat out the darkness."
That did no good either.
He said, "Shout and yell at the darkness, and order it to leave at once."
That, too, proved unsuccessful.
He said, "Light a candle."
The darkness was swept away.

This Book

This book is for anyone who is facing the darkness after the loss of a loved one and is looking for support. It's also for anyone who wants to support someone who is grieving.

My intention is to share with you what I have learned about the journey from darkness to light. This book describes my own mourning as a result of family suicides, which I will share with you, grieving heart to grieving heart. An ancient Talmudic saying goes, "Words that come from the heart enter the heart."

Regardless of the circumstances of a loved one's death, the struggle to find meaning in mourning unites us. Though I draw on teachings from the Jewish faith, as well as other religious traditions, this book is for mourners of any religion or of no religion. It transcends boundaries or labels. Death is the great common denominator, and it attests to our shared humanity. Death's darkness is a reminder that we're part of something bigger than ourselves, and this truth binds us.

Journey with me as you allow yourself to wander into the dark, confront it, and seek the sparks of possibility in the depths. Join me as a spark seeker as we cultivate those sparks into a flame, that flame into a fire, and that fire into a source of light that can illuminate our paths.

Rabbi Baruch HaLevi, DMin
February 23, 2015
Swampscott, Massachusetts

1

DARKNESS DESCENDS

The shadow is dark and the woods are cold, but they are not endless. No matter how lost you are now, you are not lost for-ever. You are findable.

–Anna White,
Mended: Thoughts on Life, Love, and Leaps of Faith

As Kisa realized, everyone has lost loved ones, and every one of us will die. It isn't personal, yet we realize that there's nothing more personal than the death of loved ones as their light dissipates or is eclipsed in the blink of an eye. The thought of losing a loved one will cause suffering, and those within the wake of loss know how personal and punishing the aftermath of death can be.

Why me? Why him? Why her? Why now? What did I do to deserve this? What did I do wrong? We ask a litany of questions as if death is unique to us alone. There's nothing more personal to us than this

SPARK SEEKERS

universal, impersonal reality. Death holds within it a paradox: it's the one thing we all share, and yet we all experience it differently. With some losses, the darkness comes across in a shade that feels manageable, while at other times, it feels like an impenetrable veil. As individualized as each loss is, regardless of the circumstances, suffering is suffering, and death is death. When it's dark, it's dark.

Wandering in Darkness

Years ago, I witnessed a solar eclipse. It was the middle of the afternoon; the sun was shining, and the birds were chirping along with all the accompanying midday rhythms. As the moon blocked out the sun, everything changed. The chirping stopped. As the noises ceased, silence eerily descended. Not knowing where to go, people froze in their tracks. Not knowing what to do, everyone looked toward the darkened mid-day sky. The eclipse transformed day into night and all I remember was feeling alone. Although I understood it intellectually, there was something mystifying, or even terrifying, about it. I felt powerless and at the mercy of the darkness.

When death's darkness comes, our usual way of living is stripped of any semblance of routine or clarity. Where there was order, there's now a feeling of chaos. The world shifts into a reality that we don't want, aren't sure how to navigate, and often feel that we can't bear. Like an eclipse, knowing about the darkness isn't the same as experiencing it. Each time is unique, and sometimes the only thing that seems real is the darkness itself.

Being a rabbi, I have had the painful privilege of being what I think of as an "emotional first responder." When I interact with an individual or family after a loss, there's always the same sense of mental, emotional, and physical shock. The wandering wounded are enveloped in a foreign darkness. Up is down, and right becomes left. The words *usual*, *typical*, and *regular* fade away, and they become disoriented within the darkness of death.

We're often like Kisa. We wander and search, desperate for miracles that undo what can't be undone. We ask questions that can't be answered, and we long to wake up and find that it was all a horrible nightmare. All we want is to return to life the way it was and have our loved ones back. We know those people won't return; our loved ones are gone, and our lives will never be the same. We grope through the dark, wondering if we will ever feel the warmth of the sun again. There's no one way to grieve. Despite a culture that often seeks to impose a timetable on grief, we wander through the aspects of mourning in our own ways. This can take days, weeks, months, or years.

Wandering is an essential part of confronting death's darkness. In the words of the thirteenth-century poet Rumi, "Out beyond ideas of wrongdoing and rightdoing, there is a field. I'll meet you there."

People in our lives often have opinions about what we should do, how we should do it, and what we should or shouldn't feel. Unless we're putting ourselves in harm's way or engaging in risky or inappropriate behavior, this isn't a time of right or wrong; it is a time of wandering.

When I met John, he was seventeen years old and in a state of shock after the sudden death of his father. He returned from school one day and learned of the tragedy in a home bustling with family, friends, the funeral director, and a rabbi—me. For an introvert like John, this collection of people would have been overwhelming even on a good day, but this was the worst day of his life. It got worse when he and his mother clashed on the appropriate way to mourn.

John's mother was an extrovert. While he needed to be alone with the news, she needed to be with people, specifically with John, and busy herself with all that needed to be done. All he wanted to do was go to his bedroom and process the tragedy by himself. She, however, wanted him to stay in the living room and participate in the funeral preparations. When she wouldn't relent, he slammed his door shut. When that didn't keep her at bay, he locked the door. The scene degenerated into screaming as she pounded on the door and demanded that he come out. No matter how much reasoning I tried, she couldn't accept his response.

Out of options, John walked out of the house. His mom was insistent that he not be alone, so I caught up with him and asked if he'd mind if I joined him. He didn't say yes, but he didn't say no. For the next hour, we walked, and he began talking about his feelings on his terms and in his own time.

John's mother loved him dearly. She wasn't right or wrong for her way of wandering into her grief, but she couldn't see that John also wasn't wrong for his response. We all respond differently to loss; we all wander according to our unique dispositions and in our own time. One way isn't better or worse, but the mourner (and his or her relationships) is potentially damaged when a wandering style is imposed or a timetable is enforced.

In the Torah, also known as the first five books of the Bible, Isaac suffers a tragic loss when his mother, Sara, dies. While his father, Abraham, finds comfort in tending to the details of Sara's funeral, Isaac walks into the fields to meditate at evening time.[2] Some people get their bearings through activity and being with others. For those like John and Isaac, direction comes through being alone, walking through fields, and wandering into the darkness.

In the literature about grief, different grieving styles are noted. Some people are referred to as "intuitive grievers." They wander into the inner world of emotions and express their feelings of loss to family, friends, counselors, or clergy. Those referred to as "instrumental grievers" wander through tasks and activities—gardening, chopping wood, or cooking—to process their grief. Some people do both by expressing their emotions at some times, and at other points, they focus on the structure of tasks.

Wandering, in its various ways, is positive. Wandering connotes a desire to find something of certainty to hold on to and find direction. Wandering may come, as it did for John's mother, through conversations with people, funeral preparations, or a list of things to be done. For others, like John, wandering may literally mean wandering fields, the beach, or the streets. A person may sit to wander through the landscape of emotions and thoughts. However it unfolds, wandering is a crucial step. It's a necessary transition period along the path from chaos to order, from powerlessness to purpose, and from darkness to light.

"I Just Saw Him"

In the initial hours and days after a loss, you run just to stand still. You hurry up just to wait. You have a thousand things that you need to do, and simultaneously it feels like nothing matters. Some people wander through the funeral preparations: the burial plot, the casket, the wake, the limousine to and from the cemetery, and the flowers and food for the guests. Other people wander by talking on the phone or receiving a flow of visitors.

In death's darkness, we lose our sense of grounding. It's as if there's no floor beneath us to carry our weights and no walls surrounding us to offer protection. Upon receiving the news about my father's death, I felt a dizzy sense of confusion. I gasped for breath and felt unanchored to time or place. I could have been alone on the summit of Mount Everest or surrounded by throngs of people in Times Square. The place where I stood emotionally was a foreign land. The darkness that descended was so quick and all encompassing that, like an eclipse, the natural order of rhythms and rules no longer existed. I was suspended between a life I knew and a new one that I couldn't grasp.

I searched my memory for the last time that I had spoken with my dad on the phone or had seen him in person. *I just spoke with him on Sunday. He can't be dead,* my mind insisted. When I called my mother, sister, and brother to break the news, they all responded similarly—gasping for air, groping to comprehend the tragedy, and focusing on the last times they had spoken with or had seen him.

I've noticed how universal this response is. We try to gain a foothold by placing our loved ones in time and space. I call this the "I Just Saw Him" response. "He can't be dead," someone will say. "I played golf with him on Tuesday." Another will utter in disbelief, "We just had dinner together last week." The "I Just Saw Him" response is a struggle to regain control and make time stop swirling. In placing the deceased on our mental calendars, we try to defy their deaths by locating them again in life. We know that it doesn't matter that we just saw our loved one—it's irrelevant and illogical—but death's darkness turns logic upside down. It's too much, too quick, and too painful. The mind begins to spin.

That's how human beings operate, and it may continue well beyond the moments or days after the loss. For weeks after my father died, I reached for the phone to call him every Sunday; that was our day to talk. As I'd begin to dial, reality would kick in, and I would remember that he was dead. At other times, his name showed up on my cell phone when it rang. It was my stepmother calling, but that's not what registered. I would sit there for a moment, trying to understand how my dead father could be calling me. On other occasions, I dreamed about my father and woke up confused as to whether my misery was real or a bad dream.

The time of learning of a loved one's death is a time of confusion consisting of more shades of gray than full darkness. For this reason, within the Jewish tradition of mourning, we're released from all time-bound commandments (daily prayer, attending synagogue, or anything having to do with time) from the moment of hearing about the death until the burial takes place. Until our loved ones are buried and the funeral is complete, we're not considered mourners; that can begin when the spinning begins to settle. In those initial moments or days, it's as if the tradition is saying that time itself is meaningless. The grief is too overwhelming, and the dark veil is impenetrable. Like Kisa, we wander through the landscape of grief.

Wandering through To-Do Lists

One of the consequences of losing our bearings is that the usual rules of how we operate no longer apply. Before the loss, time was clearly demarcated. Our jobs, responsibilities, and routines were clear on our calendars, and they told us what we needed to do and when we needed to do it. When the darkness descends, the calendar crashes and is filled with entries we never wanted and don't know how to fulfill. We're inundated with so much to attend to that life is now a to-do list. The tasks must be completed quickly in the midst of confusion and grief, and this puts us in a physically and emotionally contradictory place. Even while time stands still as we try to find our way in this new reality, in "real time" we find ourselves racing against a ticking funeral clock.

For me, this was one of the most jarring aspects of dealing with grief, and I've heard many others express the same feeling. There are preparations to be made and plans to make, delegate, communicate, and coordinate. Grief is often held at bay. If you're responsible for your loved one's funeral arrangements, there will hardly be time to acknowledge your grief.

When her mom died of a heart attack, Janie called me in a panic. She was a deeply spiritual woman, and her repertoire of practices included yoga, meditation, and prayer, all of which had carried her through trying times. She was in a shock, unable to understand how she was expected to process her grief or "find a place of spirit" within herself when there was so much to attend to. She was an only child—her father was elderly and incapacitated, and her mother had done little to prepare for her death.

I said, "Now isn't the time for grief work or spirituality. Now is a time for busy work and practicalities. When you tend to the task at hand, do so as mindfully as possible, and know that in this way, you're grieving or laying the foundation for the grief work that will come in time." This didn't eliminate anything on her to-do list, but as she shared with me later, it gave her permission to reframe the experience. It was no longer merely busy work or a distraction that kept her from doing the "real" work of mourning. It was part of mourning itself. She wanted to dive into the deep end of darkness and begin her search for sparks, but she wasn't ready. She needed to wander the sea of details and duties while she prepared to transition into the dark.

After my father's death, I was responsible for the funeral arrangements. I had to have his body transported from one state to another, neither of which I lived in. There were the added practical and logistical complications that suicide entails. When death occurs due to natural circumstances, there's so much to do. Often there's a jarring, if not perverse, feeling of being mired in minutiae like shopping for a casket—as if it were a President's Day sale—and being shown one design after another.

The waves of emotion came crashing down. I felt angry that my dad had put me in this position, although I was devastated that he was gone. I was disoriented and exhausted while wandering from obligation to expectation through a landscape of emotions. I wanted to stop and sit within the darkness, but there was too much to do before I could reach that place. There were many horrors surrounding my father's death, and being responsible for his loose ends was like salt in the wound. I had to close out his bank accounts, cancel his credit cards, and argue with his life-insurance carrier after finding out that he wasn't up to date on his premiums. He had made no funeral preparations. For me, the wandering involved coming to terms with what he had done and the implications of what he had left undone.

A Wandering River

The hours and days after a death are a slow descent into the depths of the darkness. Even months or years after emerging from it, the darkness may come rushing back out of nowhere and for no particular reason.

In her book, *On Grief and Grieving*, Elisabeth Kubler-Ross, a Swiss psychiatrist and expert in near-death experiences, proposes five stages of grief: denial, anger, bargaining, depression, and acceptance. The stages are signposts that help us to understand where we are in our grief, but they aren't necessarily linear, and we shouldn't be surprised if we experience them in varying orders or if we hardly experience a particular stage at all. Sometimes we experience one stage, assume we're done, and move on, but months later, we experience the stage again for reasons we don't understand.

The darkness is beyond your full control, and just when you think you have ascended beyond it, you find yourself back in the grief and feeling like you're at square one—like the game of Chutes and Ladders. Even when you find yourself revisiting an earlier stage, it doesn't mean that you're in the same place. You're continually evolving, gaining deeper insights about yourself and your grieving process. In the words of the philosopher Heraclitus, "No man ever steps in the same river twice, for it's not the same river, and he's not the same man."

Other theories have been proposed to understand the grieving process. Dr. William Worden, a professor of psychology and author of *Grief Counseling and Grief Therapy*, proposes a series of four tasks of mourning that may accompany the stages of grief, though they may not be parallel. The first task is to accept the reality of the loss; the second is to experience the pain of grief; the third is to adjust to an environment in which the deceased is missing; and the fourth is to emotionally relocate the deceased and move on with life by investing in new relationships.

Theresa Rando, a researcher, clinical psychologist, and author of several books on grief, offers a set of processes that people will confront as they mourn the loss of a loved one: recognizing the loss, reacting to the separation, recollecting and experiencing the deceased and the relationship, relinquishing old attachments to the deceased, readjusting to move adaptively into the new world without forgetting the old world, and reinvesting by putting emotional energy into new people and goals.[3]

While these notions of stages, tasks, and processes may be helpful during mourning, we can't look on anyone else's journey as an exact model to replicate, nor should we expect others to make the same journey we have made. The journey is uniquely ours. Everyone has an opinion about the right way to grieve, and far too many will insist that they have the answers to your sorrow: "You should cry more. You should cry less. You should talk. You should sleep. You should eat. You should keep busy. You should take it easy."

You know that well-intentioned people will tell you that they know how you feel, that they know what you're going through, and that they know your pain. They know what *they* went through, but they can't know *your* pain. There are common intersections, shared experiences, and areas where you can empathize and share. Your inner voice will guide you when you allow the chatter around you to quiet, and you hear what your heart is saying. Regardless of your best friend's well-intended advice or your neighbor's insistence that what helped her cope with the loss of her husband will help you, this is your journey. In the words of Nietzsche, "You have your way. I have my way. As for the right way, the correct way, and the only way, it does not exist."

Be gentle with yourself without expectations of how your process will unfold. Allow yourself time to tend to the mundane details. Give yourself permission to feel whatever you're feeling or not feel whatever you're not feeling. Know that the equilibrium of space and time has been torn out from under you. Give yourself permission to be wherever you need to be. As things settle and you have the time to sit and absorb what you're going through, being within the darkness in any way that suits you is enough. There's a beautiful Zen proverb that reads as follows:

Sitting quietly
doing nothing,
spring comes,
and the grass grows by itself.

Rather than trying to force the process, allowing it to be what it is in the moment leads to growth in and of itself.

During this time, relinquish your expectations of what is normal and your assumptions about what should be. Your world has dramatically changed, and you need time and space to get your bearings. It's all part of the journey across the landscape of grief. It's preparing you for what is coming and the magnitude of your loss. As you move from dusk to night, remind yourself that wandering is natural while you take in a new reality without your loved one by your side.

Survival Is Enough

Recently I was watching a survival show where a guy was dropped into the wilderness with only a knife, some random gadgets, and a will to survive. As the sun was setting, he scrambled to build a shelter and start a fire so that he could make it through the night. The next day he would set forth to find his way home. In those early moments alone in the wilderness, as dusk was turning to darkness and the dangers of the night loomed, he had one job: survive.

The time between the death of a loved one and the funeral or memorial service is, in many ways, like being dropped off deep in the wilderness. We know that the darkness is coming, but we haven't yet allowed it to set in. Amid the rushing around, the riptide of grief looms. It's held back for a while as we tend to the tasks at hand, such as the wake, funeral, condolence meal, or *shiva* (the seven-day period of mourning in a Jewish home). When the darkness sets in, we remind ourselves that wherever we are is OK. Right now, we're surviving amid the searing pain, and right now, survival is enough.

2

DEMONS IN THE DARK

We can easily forgive a child who is afraid of the dark; the real tragedy of life is when men are afraid of the light.

—Plato

Some of my first memories as a child revolve around bedtime rituals. After washing, brushing my teeth, and saying my prayers, there was the inevitable "chair ritual." In my bedroom, I had a toddler-sized table-and-chair set that my parents insisted were in the shape of a puppy and a kitten. As innocent as that may sound right now, I assure you that when the lights went out, those chairs turned into monsters. Every evening, I made my dad lay the chairs down on the floor, and if he forgot, at some point in the night, I cried out for him to come and rescue me. "There are monsters in my bedroom!" I would scream. He had to lay the chairs down and—as a precautionary measure—turn on the lights.

Nighttime Rituals

Isn't it interesting that most of us have some version of this type of memory? All of my children have a variation on this theme. For one of my kids, monsters lived under the bed, and for the other, the boogeyman lived in the closet. For another, there was no boogeyman, but he lived by an eleventh commandment, "Thy door shalt remain open"—his and mine—"all night." The youngest one looked up to his three older siblings, and he inherited a combination of their fears.

From the time we're old enough to be aware of the dark, we're afraid of it. As we get older, we believe that we outgrow this childish fear. Our fear of darkness is still filled with monsters, but they're not the kind of childhood monsters we imagined living under our beds. In the words of the novelist Stephen King, "Monsters are real, and ghosts are real too. They live inside us, and sometimes, they win."[4] When death's darkness sets in, no matter who we are, no matter how fearless we believe ourselves to be, we resort to primal, eternal fears of the dark. It's human, but most of us don't want to acknowledge how afraid we can be.

Finding ourselves surrounded by our fears of the dark and knowing they won't be dispelled by the flip of a switch, we often deny the experience as a way to survive. Denial of death's darkness is such a universal phenomenon that Kubler-Ross identified this first stage of grief as a natural response to the loss of a loved one. Denial can serve the constructive purpose of offering wanderers the time needed to adjust to a new reality. We survive each day by going through the motions of living when we feel empty and lost. When we deny something, we aren't yet ready to acknowledge it or face it.

During the early stages of loss, wandering in denial offers a way to make out the looming shadows as we adjust to the dark. However, wandering for too long in denial becomes a way of avoiding the darkness, which demands to be entered. The monsters never go away on their own. When we wander for too long, we fall down a slippery slope and move from wandering to running away from the monsters we fear. There comes a point within every journey when wandering can shift from constructive to destructive. Wandering toward the darkness may sometimes turn into running away from it and pretending it's something that can be avoided. Wolfelt notes, "Without doubt, the grief journey requires contemplation and turning inward. In other words, it requires depression, anxiety, and loss of control. It requires going into the wilderness."[5]

Many try to avoid that dark wilderness by clinging to the belief that if they deny its existence, they can move on without holding the pain of grief. I've seen this happen on many occasions with those I guide. I've experienced it myself when dealing with loss. I witnessed this within my own family, particularly with my father, who spent a lifetime running from the monsters and denying the darkness. Those demons eventually proved to be fatal for him. They destroyed my grandmother and father and caused my family to sink farther into the depths of despair. Monsters don't go away—they merely lie dormant, waiting to reemerge.

Unholy Silence

I was born in an idyllic setting with a doting family, wonderful teachers, a nurturing and close-knit community, and plenty of friends and activities. It was an era of innocence.

One day, my innocence ended, and my family's life was shattered—my paternal grandmother had killed herself. No one in my family would ever be the same. What began in that moment and lasted until the writing of this book, spanning more than a quarter of a century, has become a central preoccupation of my personal and professional journey. However, what led up to that moment began decades before. The years of family members trying to suppress the demons or deny their existence allowed those demons to fester and grow; eventually they consumed us.

We've all heard the saying that "silence is golden." Another type of silence, which I call "unholy silence," is anything but golden. The Genevan philosopher Jean-Jacques Rousseau said, "Absolute silence leads to sadness. It is the image of death." Unholy silences create chaos and bring us anything but calm. They are those moments when something could have and should have been said but wasn't. The era in which my father came of age and my grandmother came undone was, in many ways, a time of unholy silence.

In previous generations, when it came to acceptable subject matters for conversation, a tremendous amount was deemed unsuitable. Illness and disease, sex, divorce, and abortion were all in the realm of unholy silence, but nothing was more taboo than mental illness.

My grandmother was a victim of such silence. She spent the better part of her life battling depression in a world that didn't understand what she was fighting. She endured every treatment offered at the time, and electroconvulsive therapy—as it was administered in those days—left her a shadow of her former self. As destructive as her depression was, the silence surrounding it visited the greatest suffering on her and our family.

While she was alive, I remember asking my grandfather and my father questions about her illness and being rebuked. I was reminded that it wasn't something we talked about and wasn't to be brought up again. In silence, I watched my grandmother degenerate in body, mind, and spirit. I remember visiting her, sitting with her, and holding her soft hands; I remember the smooth stroke of her cheek against mine when she kissed me. At the same time, I'll never forget the lifelessness in her eyes as she sat smoking cigarette after cigarette. More than the suffocating smoke that swirled in the midst, I remember the choking, oppressive silence.

In many ways, this unwillingness to confront her and my family's darkness made the darkness ominous and resulted in what came next. After years of depression, my grandmother couldn't endure any more. When I was fifteen years old, she took my grandfather's gun, proceeded to her basement, and shot herself through the heart. In a matter of moments she was dead; her monsters were silenced. However, the darkness, the monsters, and the devastating silence she left in the aftermath for her husband, children, and grandchildren were staggering, and it would lead my family, particularly my dad, to try to outrun the monsters for two decades.

On the day she killed herself, my grandfather found her and called my dad. He raced over to discover his mother dead in a pool of blood.

As this was happening, I was arriving home from school. I had a learner's permit, which allowed me to drive to and from school. While driving down the street, I felt a sense of foreboding. There were too many cars in my driveway for an ordinary weekday afternoon. When I jumped out of my car, my mother confirmed my fears. "Your grandmother is dead. Your father is over there now," she told me. The rest is blurry. There were my mother's pleas to stay home and my defiance as I (illegally) raced across town to arrive at the scene as the paramedics were carting my grandmother away. I remember thinking, *That's my grandmother under that sheet?* as the paramedics put her into the ambulance. I barreled down into the basement before anyone could stop me and witnessed the aftermath of what had taken place. The sight of the blood on the floor and on my father's clothes, the putrid smell in the air, and the look on my father's face are burned into my mind. I felt dazed and confused, unable to process my thoughts.

What I don't remember in those hours and days after her suicide was my grandfather. I think it was because his silence wasn't a stoic silence but a broken, absent silence. He was a decent man but far from an emotionally healthy or whole person, even before my grandmother's death. He had been chipped away over decades of dealing with her mental illness. In many ways, he was alone in his darkness. Although he lived another fifteen years, in essence he died that day alongside his wife and was unwilling to face her darkness or his own.

After we emerged from the basement, trying to absorb the reality of what happened, my father shattered the silence. He went from pale and detached to alive and furious. He grabbed me and almost dragged me out of the house to get away from the horror of the scene. We got into his car, and he moved from silence to sobbing. He reached across to the passenger side and pulled me into the nape of his neck, holding me tightly. I'll never forget the strength of his hands as he forcefully, but lovingly, squeezed me. I can't forget, as much as I'd like to, the way his fingers gripped my neck and hair as he let out a primal cry that I would only hear one other time in my life. "*Why? Why? Why?*" he screamed in broken sobs as tears ran down his face.

I have no idea how long this lasted, but I knew in that moment more than my grandmother had died. This was the moment that I lost my grandmother, my grandfather, my dad, and my youth. I felt the darkness descending in a way that I knew would forever change our family, especially my dad. He may have been holding onto me tightly in that car, but the truth was that he was barely holding onto his own life. In that moment, he began trying to escape the demons that he couldn't bear. They had been unleashed by his mother, and they left him terrified and confused within the dark.

Silence and Society

Fast-forward more than thirty years, and you'll find much has changed when it comes to the culture of silence. Now virtually no conversation is off limits. Whether it's in the private or the public realm, you can talk about anything, but the silence around death still pervades.

Emily, a middle-aged woman, came to speak to me about the loss of her husband, Jim. On a morning like any other, he headed to work while she was still sleeping, just as he had done hundreds of times before. He never arrived at work. He was involved in a fatal car crash, and she never saw him again. She was eight months pregnant, and her son never met his father.

Emily did what she needed to do to raise her son. Those around her thought she was doing fine, but when I met her nearly two decades after her husband's death, I saw a double tragedy. Her son was eighteen years old and preparing to head off to college. His nearing departure unlocked the emotional rooms that Emily had sealed off years ago. She had shut down those emotions because her parents told her she must be stoic and "get over" her grief so that her son would have a happy childhood. Her in-laws left the country, telling her that seeing her and their grandson would be too painful for them to bear. They moved forward without looking back and cut themselves off from her. Her friends, as attentive as they were in the early months, had moved on with their lives. The expressions of, "We're here for you, whatever you need," gave way to not-so-subtle expressions of exasperation with her "prolonged" grieving. A year had passed, more than the time they deemed sufficient for such an attractive and available young woman as Emily to continue living in her gloom. One friend, unbeknownst to Emily, even signed her up for an online dating service to mark the first anniversary of Jim's death.

The Emilys of the world, whose reality defies the norm—most twentysomethings aren't widows or widowers—have legions of painful stories of hurtful comments and actions made by family and friends. In the absence of compassionate, unconditional support, Emily and others like her learn that few people want to hear about their pain. They are told in subtle or not-so-subtle ways to pack up their grief and move out from the darkness and back into life.

Emily did what she thought she had to do. She packed up Jim's things, packed up their memories, packed up her grief, and moved on with her life, believing that the monsters were gone and a new life had begun. Her son's graduation brought it all back, or perhaps uncovered what had always been there. The monsters had never gone away. They were waiting for her and returned with a vengeance. They are never defeated, not with unholy silence or with false light.

Emily isn't alone. Countless widows, widowers, and survivors of all types of loss are prematurely told to pack up their grief, run from the demons, and get back to life. As a culture, we push death away. We rarely make room for grief in all of its expressions, for the darkness that descends or for meaningful conversations about it.

Some congregants said to me, "Rabbi, we'd like you to visit our mother as long as you promise not to tell her or let on to the fact she's dying." Their mother was ninety-five years old. She had been battling cancer for years and was in hospice, yet I was supposed to tiptoe around the subject of death.

"What shall I speak to her about?" I asked.

"Whatever you want, just not death."

If this attitude weren't so prevalent, it would be laughable. We all have the right to decide what is best for ourselves or family members who are unable to make such decisions; however, as I explained to the family, discomfort with death is hardly an excuse not to confront it. This elderly woman was lucid. She was strong, and she knew that she was dying. The problem wasn't the woman but her children and their fear of death.

I said to them, "Every person has a right to a dignified life, and everyone has a right to a dignified death."

Outside of exceptional circumstances, Alzheimer's disease, for instance, there's no dignity in thinking that you're tired when, in fact, you're dying. Speaking the truth is part of the process of accepting the truth and working with it in a way that serves both the dying person and the loved ones. However, too many of us don't want to talk about loss after a loved one dies. We don't want to talk about it while we or our loved ones are alive.

If silence permeates death in general, nowhere is this truer than when it comes to suicide. There's such a shroud of silence surrounding the subject that few are aware that suicide is now the leading cause of "injury death" in America. In the United States, military suicide has reached epidemic proportions. In 2012, more US soldiers died by suicide than were killed by enemy combatants, and veterans killed themselves at a rate of one every sixty-five minutes.[6]

Tragically, this and other statistics surrounding suicide seem to be on an upward trend. A recent series of articles reported that in this country, every form of preventable death is on the decline except suicide. Murder, car deaths, heart disease, AIDS, and deaths related to alcohol and drugs are all on the decline, but the incidence of suicide is skyrocketing. Suicide was responsible for more deaths in 2012 than drug abuse, alcohol abuse, and smoking combined. It outpaces heart disease and murder, and yet we rage at these other forms of death.[7] We throw money and medical research at them, as we should, but when it comes to suicide, we're silent. We're terrified that if we pay attention to it or talk about it, that will make it worse.

I had the painful responsibility of officiating at the funeral of a twenty-two-year-old woman named Brooke who had killed herself. It's difficult enough officiating under such circumstances, but it's even more challenging when the deceased's loved ones don't want the word *suicide* mentioned or any allusion made to the fact the person took his or her life. Brooke's parents took it a step further. In spite of the fact Brooke had attempted suicide multiple times, they wanted me to say that she died of a drug allergy. Everyone knew it was a suicide, but it was as if admitting that would unleash the demons when, in fact, sharing the truth would release the demons. I couldn't stand there and speak words that were blatantly false. All we have is the truth, and I believed that corroborating their story would add to their darkness. In the end, we agreed that I would avoid the topic entirely. Better to live in denial than rewrite the truth. Maybe someday they will change their minds and truly lay their daughter to rest, but I believe that process will entail speaking the truth about their daughter's death.

This situation isn't unique to Brooke's family. We try to protect ourselves and our loved ones from the pain of loss. We continue to try to outrun the monsters, but this only fuels the demons. We move farther and farther into the unholy silence.

Margaret, a woman in her seventies whose parents died forty years earlier, shared with me that she couldn't mention her parents' names without breaking into tears. Far be it from me to impose a time frame on someone's sorrow, but no matter how you slice it, that is more than a healthy amount of grieving time. When I suggested that it might be time for her to seek grief counseling to move through her heartache, she quit the synagogue in indignation.

Barry and Janet, also in their seventies, asked if I would officiate at the renewal of their wedding vows. While preparing for the big day, I asked them why they never had children. They shared that they had had a son, but he died as an infant, and they could never go through that pain again. They couldn't even say his name. They feared that doing so would unleash the floodgates of grief. They not only buried their son all those years ago they buried their abilities to communicate and process their grief.

Sophie was a forty-five-year-old child of Holocaust survivors. She came to me to help her get through the suffering she endured due to an eating disorder. Knowing that anorexia nervosa and bulimia have been associated with children of Holocaust survivors, I suggested that we talk about the issue.[8] A look of terror crossed her face. No one in her family ever spoke about her parents' experience. The atrocities were too great, and the losses were too severe. She was an only child with no aunts or uncles—they were all murdered in Germany—and she was taught not to talk about these dark horrors. She understandably did what so many others tormented by death's darkness have done: she carried the unholy silence from one generation to the next. The unspoken grief manifested in the language of a body unwilling to be nourished. Because of her eating disorder, her body resembled the unmentionable: the living corpses of those who died in concentration camps. She accepted the unholy silence but at a great cost. Her emaciated body spoke the unspoken. In the absence of communication, the unholy silence speaks.

The Cancer of Silence

After my grandmother killed herself, my father put himself back together as best as he was able. After those initial days of intense grief, he seemed to suck it up and deal with his darkness by getting back to his routines, including work. Like many people in the aftermath of a loss, he believed he was too busy for grief. He was busy raising a family, building a business, and playing his part within a community. I think he believed that he was doing us a favor by not delving into the darkness. He focused on putting his head down, providing for his family, and living by the mantra, "Everything is fine." This determination carried him forward for a while, and to an outsider looking in, everything appeared fine.

The unprocessed guilt, grief, confusion, and anger over his mother's suicide were growing louder in his soul. Roughly a decade later, he had a nervous breakdown. The years of suffering in silence proved too much for him. He collapsed and required psychiatric hospitalization. I remember talking with him in those days and the look of absence and hopelessness in his eyes. Not knowing how to reach him, I wrote out the lyrics to his favorite song, Simon and Garfunkel's "The Sound of Silence," and gave them to him. He may have heard those words a hundred times, but I don't believe he ever truly listened to them. I was losing him, and I knew it. All I wanted was for him to listen to me, to the doctors, or to someone, but his darkness was, indeed, his old friend; it echoed through his soul. Although he lived for another decade, cobbling a life out of the broken fragments, in many ways the dad I loved and the man everyone knew was gone.

In the years that followed, he continued to run from his dark demons. He eventually left my mother and sabotaged his thriving business. He pulled away from his community, turning his back on lifelong relationships and severing ties with dear friends. He moved away from his hometown and disappeared to a new city where he banked on anonymity—a life free from expectation or obligation.

He remarried, started a new line of work, created a new community of friends, and changed his name. His legal name was Sheldon. In his childhood, he was called Shelly and later Shel. To him, *Shelly* probably represented the innocence of youth. I imagine that he associated this with a time when his mother was whole, before her darkness set in. *Shel* probably symbolized the span of darkened years, his mother's depression, her suicide, and his years of suffering. Shel was a man who built a life, created a business, acquired worldly possessions, and sacrificed for those around him. All the while, the Shelly within him went unheeded and unheard.

When he left the psychiatric hospital, he refused to be called Shel. From then on, he was Shelly. In changing his name, he probably believed that he was exorcising his demons and changing his destiny.

The life my father was making was built on quicksand; the faster he built, the faster he sank. In leaving behind his home, he began to exhibit what the philosopher Will Herberg calls, "Cut flower culture."[9] Although he seemed to be fine, even prospering in some ways, in the end, like cut flowers, it was an illusion. The moment he extricated himself from the soil where he had roots, unfinished business, and a darkness that he refused to enter, he began to wither and move closer to death.

This isn't to say that we can't start new lives, but burying grief, denying suffering, and running from death's darkness to a new place merely offers the old life in a new location. It's like the Buddhist saying, "Wherever you go, there you are."

Wolfelt notes the following:

Quick fixes may in fact achieve repression of normal symptoms of grief. But at what price? Repressed thoughts and feelings always return to haunt the human psyche. If we try to resist the overwhelming power of grief, it will inevitably express itself through fallout consequences...I like to refer to these consequences as living in the "shadow of the ghosts" of grief.[10]

My dad didn't deal with his darkness. He packed it up and took it with him, all the while denying that it was there. He believed that he had overcome it. The darkness wasn't only still there; it was all that was there. He filled his life with shortcuts and quick fixes that offered no real illumination or healing. His darkness was growing beneath the surface and increasingly dominating him.

Darkness denied is darkness delayed. Sooner or later, it comes out with even greater force. The darkness my father spent his life avoiding washed over him like a tidal wave. The monsters swallowed him alive. No matter how much, how hard, or how fast he danced, it was never enough. As a child, I called to him at night to save me from the monsters lurking in my bedroom. As an adult, I watched him succumb to his own monsters. Neither he nor I knew how to turn on the light and save him from the demons that would no longer be denied.

The pull to avoid the dark and the pain is strong. As Scottish psychiatrist R. D. Laing says, "Pain in this life is not avoidable, but the pain we create avoiding pain is avoidable." There are many ways that people attempt to avoid the reality of death, and yet in doing so, the pain that occurs when death comes is often magnified.

When We Don't Prepare

We all know that we will die. One would think that this would mean that we would prepare for our deaths. There are those who tragically die at young ages, but most of us who live to a ripe, old age don't make preparations for when the time comes. End-of-life experts estimate that only 20 to 30 percent of Americans have advanced directives,[11] and less than 33 percent of Americans pre-plan for their funerals.[12] When we don't address end-of-life issues, we add financial and emotional strains on our loved ones in what is an already unbearable time.

Mr. Grossman was the patriarch of his family. He spent a lifetime providing for his wife, children, grandchildren, and community. He and Mrs. Grossman were representative of an era when couples had clearly defined roles in their marriages and their duties to their families; they often didn't speak to each other about what the other was tending to. It was assumed that each person was taking care of his or her respective responsibilities. Mrs. Grossman took care of the domestic duties, her husband's daily needs, and the day-to-day tasks of raising a family. Mr. Grossman took care of the financial issues while making sure that his wife and children were provided for and secure. This was why it was shocking for the family to discover upon his sudden death that Mr. Grossman had done nothing about his end-of-life issues. He had no medical directives; his will was out of date; he had no funeral arrangements; and he didn't even own burial plots. Mrs. Grossman and the kids were caught off guard.

The family scrambled to buy burial plots, find legal and financial documents, and gather the other information needed when a loved one dies. It took a toll on them, but they rose to the occasion and did what needed to be done to get through their painful ordeal. In not planning for his death, Mr. Grossman added burdens to his family that he likely never intended.

I sit with families as they gather at the hospital bedsides of their loved ones and decide on the spot what Mom or Dad would want by way of medical intervention or palliative care. I have watched families be ripped apart when trying to decipher their loved ones' wishes or battle over what to do, who should decide, and how to resolve a split decision. Many of us say little about this monumental event or make few if any preparations for it.

More people are talking about death in the sense of preventable deaths. There have been campaigns to educate people about early detection screenings for cancer, the need for good nutrition and exercise to prevent heart disease, the warning signs of a stroke, and the life-saving importance of preventative health care. This is necessary and welcome work in helping people live longer, healthier lives, but despite the campaigns, little is said in terms of death as a reality that must be reckoned with. There's a Zen Buddhist prayer said at the conclusion of the day as a reminder that life is fleeting and death is waiting in the wings: "Let me respectfully remind you—life and death are of supreme importance. Time swiftly passes, and opportunity is lost. Each of us should strive to awaken. Take heed. Do not squander your life."

In our society, a death can be reported across newspaper headlines, become the top story of the evening news, or dominate Facebook pages, but in terms of talking about death as an inevitability and using this knowledge to make our lives richer, we remain silent. In the community where I'm a rabbi, we have made repeated attempts to host end-of-life symposia to discuss and plan for death and its concomitant issues. Few people show up. Some seniors will come, but their adult children fail to join them, regardless of the fact they aren't getting any younger themselves. This is a highly educated and successful group, yet when it comes to death, none of that matters. It's as if they believe that if they don't talk about it, it isn't real. Instead of showing up, they go to the golf course, the movies, the beach—anywhere other than a place that makes them confront their mortality. Closing their eyes to it won't change the inevitable. Sometimes it takes a lesson about what can happen when no end-of-life preparations are made for people to open their eyes.

For many in my community, that realization involved a woman named Joy. When I arrived as rabbi at my congregation, I was warned about Joy. The name didn't suit her, because she wasn't the smiling sort. She was definitely not joyful. Even though she stood five feet tall and weighed maybe a hundred pounds, everyone tiptoed around her. I joined the rank and file and soon took marching orders from her, steering clear when I could tell that she was grumpy. I learned to quit arguing with her even when I was right.

Joy was getting on in years. She was widowed more than a quarter of a century earlier and had no children. She had never remarried and had no companionship outside of her synagogue. As difficult as she could be, the congregation loved her and depended on her as much as she depended on them. She was in charge of scheduling who led the daily services, and we knew that if one of us were crossed off that list, we had crossed her. Outside of the synagogue, except for distant family, she had nobody.

I was approached by a congregant who wanted to share with me her concerns. She said, "Joy is well into her nineties. She has no end-of-life preparations, no healthcare proxy, and no medical directives. She has no will. Will you speak with her and get her to prepare?" (No one really knew how old she was; she was probably closer to one hundred.)

I was apprehensive. If Joy had gotten this far without taking care of such issues, I doubted she'd listen to the new rabbi that she sometimes referred to as "the little *pischer*," which means a nobody or an inexperienced person. She would sometimes say to me, "Rabbi, I have problems older than you." Still, it was my duty to try.

I tried to bring up the issue in conversation, in person and in writing, but it was to no avail. Every time I got close to the subject of death, dying, or funeral arrangements, Joy made it clear that those subjects were off limits.

I didn't make my case with the conviction and urgency that the subjects demanded, and then it was too late. Joy suffered a stroke, and our worst fears—and probably hers, although no one knew because she never spoke about these things—came true. She spent the next month in the intensive-care unit on ventilators and other life-sustaining machines. Her synagogue friends, doctors, lawyer, and rabbi were powerless to do much of anything.

A hospital ethics panel was convened. Lawyers and judges got involved, and experts were brought in to advise. As her rabbi, I was responsible for educating the panel on the Jewish view of end-of-life issues. The decision was made—not by her family, her community, or her rabbi but by a bureaucratic healthcare system—that her life support should be unplugged. This should have been her decision to address while she was alive. Because she wouldn't discuss death, and because I—and many others—was afraid of pushing harder to break through the silence, everyone paid the price.

After Joy died, new struggles began: funeral arrangements, cemetery plots, liquidating and selling her estate, and locating her next of kin for their inheritances. It was uncanny how her family was nonexistent when it came to dealing with *mishagas* (mayhem) surrounding her death but, when it came to dispersing her assets, they quickly made themselves known. Many decent people became involved out of the goodness of their hearts. They tried as best they could to fulfill Joy's wishes without knowing exactly what they might be. Every step of the way, everyone involved, from friends and community members to doctors, judges, and myself, was worse for the experience. The process dragged on for years, leaving many people depleted. It was demoralizing and disheartening.

All these years later, if you mention Joy in the synagogue, almost everyone thinks of the same thing: the lesson learned in how *not* to approach death and why we must break the silence about end-of-life issues. Joy's death served as a cautionary tale, but despite the lessons learned, many people still resist entering this conversation and purposeful planning.

Scrambling to make these decisions for a loved one at the time of death not only causes duress and family tension, but it delays the real work at hand: grieving. It's perhaps the hardest work with which we will ever engage. It's an added burden on our loved ones when we don't plan for it and let our wishes be known, and we owe it to our loved ones and ourselves to take care of these decisions.

The more we can attend to the details surrounding how we want to die and what we want in the aftermath, the more we allow our loved ones to hold their own grief without added burdens. The more we take responsibility for our monsters in the dark, whatever those demons might be, and the more we're willing to face the truth of our own mortality, the better we're able to live our lives more fully and lovingly.

3

THE VOID DANCE

People spend entire lifetimes trying to avoid the things that have already happened.

—Sylvia Hartmann

We live in a world of avoidance, or what Rabbi Marc Gafni calls "a void dance."[13] It's an attempt to dance around the darkness instead of entering it to discover the healing sparks of light. We attempt the dance in endless ways, but in the end, the attempts are in vain. Sooner or later, the dancing will stop, and we will have to confront the void. Like my father, we may even be swallowed by its pull. The longer we delay, the deeper and darker the void grows, making it that much more dangerous when we fall in.

The Void Dance

I have witnessed this void dance in my family, and I have watched it play out in the lives of many others I know and guide.

When someone is dying or has died, being a rabbi, I make a call like the one I recently made to Chad.

Chad was a middle-aged man who was close with his father. His dad died after a short struggle with cancer, and I assumed that Chad and the family would be distraught.

I called him. "Chad, I'm so sorry to hear about your dad. Is there anything I can do?"

"No, we're fine."

"Really? I imagine this was difficult to find out. I'd be happy to come over and talk with you, Cindy, your mom, or whomever would like to talk."

"I appreciate that, Rabbi. I really do. Truly, we're fine. We'll call you if we need you."

I also made a call to Mr. and Mrs. Cohen. I learned through the grapevine that their son, a man in his late sixties, had died by suicide a few weeks prior. The person who told me shared this news in a hushed whisper. Because neither the Cohens nor anyone in the community told their synagogue about the death, I assumed that they didn't want any attention drawn to their tragedy. Nonetheless, I wanted to make a call.

"Mr. Cohen, it's Rabbi HaLevi."

"Yes?" He replied as if I was calling for the capital campaign.

"I just heard about your son."

"Yes. He died," he said nonchalantly, as if it had happened years ago.

"I know. I'm so sorry. Is there anything I can do? Can I come over and visit?"

"No, we're fine."

"Are you sure? It's no problem. I can come over anytime. Although I don't know what it's like to lose a son, I lost a father in the same way," I said. I skirted around the *S* word since he hadn't brought it up.

"Yes, I know. We're fine," he said with a hint of annoyance.

"Well, if Mrs. Cohen wants to talk, can I leave my number?"

"No, that won't be necessary. She's fine, too. So nice of you to call. Bye."

Mourners can move through the grieving process and get to a place where they are "fine" and able to bear the weight of the darkness. Learning to face death and move through the darkness with resolve is part of what it means to return to a new reality where we truly experience a sense of being fine. However, there's a world of difference between saying, "I'm fine," and feeling it. Every premature "I'm fine" conversation is a sure sign that beneath the surface, the monsters of grief are lurking. No amount of denial can keep them at bay forever.

You can arrive at a place of renewed purpose and vitality after loss, and even because of it, but there's nothing *fine* about the Herculean journey through grief. It's purposeful but painful. It's profound but hard. It's meaningful but agonizing, and the one thing it is not is *fine*. Until we start confronting the darkness by entering that void and seeing what is there, we will never truly be fine. We leave ourselves open to the consequences of ignoring a festering wound.

Communal Dancing

While the void dance is often individual, it can also be danced communally. As a society, there are no shortages of ways that we dance around the void of death. One societal void dance takes place in how little we allow death to be seen in the marketplace. When was the last time you saw a billboard, corporate sponsorship, or TV ad for a funeral home, hospice facility, or death-related business? It's as if this industry doesn't exist, but in fact, it's booming. In the United States, the funeral market is estimated to be worth $20.7 billion annually.[14] Despite this, our culture has adopted an attitude that if we don't pay attention to this area of life, it doesn't exist. We step into this dance through the language used for the funeral as we talk about the "departed" who has "passed on" or been "laid to rest." No matter how much we distance ourselves from this issue with softened terms or try to keep it out of the public eye, we can never out dance the reality of death's darkness once it has descended.

In other parts of the world, the reality of movement between life and death is more transparent. In Southeast Asia, for example, the body is carried through the streets en route to a cremation *ghat;* the body is burned, and the ashes are swept into the holy body of water below. While family and friends accompany their loved ones and tend to the cremation ritual, others in their midst are busy living their lives, selling their wares, and going about their day. Life and death are bound together in a way unseen within American culture.

An older congregant named Shirley came to my office after the death of her husband, Lou. She was understandably sad, but what bothered her most was seeing her husband's body. His mouth was open, and it was more than she could bear. She begged the nurse to close his mouth, but the nurse explained that there was no way to keep his mouth closed in his state. She had to leave the room, and the image wouldn't leave her mind.

Not so long ago in our culture, death was an organic part of life. When loved ones died at home, young and old, family, friends, neighbors, and community were frequently exposed to the unsanitized aspects of death. Today, on cultural and individual levels, we're unaccustomed to seeing death and are uncomfortable with the messiness. When we try to hide death or run away in fear, we often lose access to that which will heal us.

Death holds a powerful grip on our minds, emotions, and spirits. Prolonged void dancing only strengthens this grip. No matter how hard we dance, the void of death's darkness is there, pulling us toward it. The only way to dispel the darkness is to face its painful truths and learn its harrowing insights. In the words of American essayist and novelist Edward Abbey, "You can't study the darkness by flooding it with light." We can and must dispel the darkness, but that can happen only when we take a leap of faith into the void, understand it, and move through it. Until we do, we exhaust ourselves without coming to a sense of inner peace and rest. The longer we dance around the void, the longer it will take us to move through the darkness and return to a place of light.

The Chopped-Liver Dance

When death descends, there are a million details to attend to in preparation for the funeral. Whether it's the wake, the funeral, the condolence meal, or the shiva home, it's easy to get caught in the whirlwind of the void dance. These rituals allow us to stop planning, rushing around, and preparing for the funeral and to start preparing for the grief. This is our only job, and yet the bereaved often confuse this job with being the host or hostess. In Judaism, the point of a shiva home is for the mourners to do nothing, to be tended to and waited upon, and to be supported in their grief. Even though it may be in their own homes, the guests become the hosts, and the bereaved family members are the guests. That is the theory, but in reality, we often become like Mrs. Schwartz.

A few years back, Mrs. Schwartz lost her husband of more than fifty years. She was distraught, but you would never have guessed it by looking at her after the funeral.

"Mrs. Schwartz, you look amazing," people told her. Her hair, her makeup, and her house were perfect. Everything was perfect except for the chopped liver.

Knowing how much her husband loved chopped liver, one woman asked in jest, "Mrs. Schwartz, where is the chopped liver?" You could see a light bulb go off in her head. How could she have forgotten the chopped liver? It was her husband's favorite dish, and no one could make it for him like she did. The ingredients were all there in her fridge, but in the tumult of the day, she had forgotten to make it. As soon as this woman finished her sentence, Mrs. Schwartz was in the kitchen.

"No, Mrs. Schwartz," the woman pleaded, "I was just kidding."

It was too late. No matter how much anyone begged Mrs. Schwartz to stop, assured her it wasn't important, or pleaded with her to sit and rest, there was no stopping her. As she frantically chopped and prepared the ingredients, one could see the "chopped-liver dance" carrying her further from the void. She wasn't making chopped liver. In her mind, she was keeping Mr. Schwartz alive.

If everything in that shiva home was perfect—and she believed it was her job to make it so—the darkness would be kept at bay. Mrs. Schwartz was terrified of the dark, so she hid behind cosmetic and culinary perfection. It wasn't perfect; her husband was dead, regardless of how much chopped liver she busied herself with. Once she stopped dancing, primping, and cooking around the void, she would have to face the darkness.

Line Dancing

Back in the day, line dancing was a country-western phenomenon. Today, it's something else entirely. Phone lines, cable lines, and Internet lines offer an unprecedented number of ways to connect. These lines link to smartphones, tablets, and computer screens, and each flickering screen has the potential to pull us away from the dark. In virtual time, we have another dimension to grapple with when it's time to face the void.

E-mail, texting, and social-media websites are a gift and, in some ways, can be extremely helpful when coping with the death of a loved one. On numerous occasions, I've been with families in hospice settings or at hospital bedsides who used online updates or group e-mails to keep those who were concerned up to date. For the family and the community, it's a great tool for sharing information. It's also a useful way to alert the community to someone's death, share details of the funeral, and direct donations.

In my synagogue, we draw on the gift of technology and offer the option of webcasting the funeral. Although it may sound impersonal, I can assure you that it's the opposite. I've done funerals for family members who couldn't be in the same location. In one case, a husband had died while his wife was in hospice care on the other side of the country. She had the opportunity to share this sacred occasion, and in many ways, it was both a celebration of their life together and a way for her to say good-bye to her family.

Technology can be a gift, but on many occasions, I have witnessed it devolve in the wake of death into an attempt to artificially illuminate the dark. The e-mails, texts, and Facebook comments become distractions and ways to escape reality. In the depths of sorrow, how can you respond to a text message that reads, "SS4URL," so sorry for your loss? Friends may use social networks to give virtual nods of sympathy without having to enter the reality of death's darkness. What is a mourner to make of Facebook friends hitting the "Like" button when she announces her loved one's death? It's easy to find a constant line of virtual people ready to offer comfort, and comfort is crucial to our journeys through the void, but virtual support isn't the same as real-life support. Facebook "likes" aren't the same as holding a hand or giving a hug. The shorthand of texting condolences is a poor substitute for what is needed in a time of grief.

For the mourner, the almost intoxicating experience of texting, e-mailing, Facebooking, tweeting, or blogging about a loved one's death, as important as it is, can become an eternal escape from the work of real communication. I discovered this shadow side of the Internet after my dad died. For hours, I sat and blogged about his death. While initially I viewed this as a constructive way to process what I was going through, in hindsight I realized that, on many levels, it was a way to dance around the void. Blogging brought with it a level of expectation and perfection. I would write and rewrite, proof and critique, imagining a cyberspace audience that was moved by my words. I now see that I was dancing around my grief and hiding behind the so-called perfection of those words. I see this often when the bereaved prepare eulogies for their loved ones, writing and rewriting toward an imagined idea of perfection. It becomes about speaking the perfect words as opposed to using those words to express their grief. Even the best-intended activities have the potential to become dances around the void.

Our demanding online communities are high-speed connections. With every Facebook post, responses are anticipated. E-mail can, and should, wait, but not everyone is willing to let a mourner off the hook from responding promptly. As much as technology is a gift, it can be used to virtually connect without ultimately connecting. It can be a high-tech void dance.

The online world itself can become a tremendous burden. Jane was devastated when her mother died suddenly from a brain aneurism. She and her mom were the heart of her family, and they made sure that everyone stayed up to date with one another. Mother and daughter were take-charge women who could tackle any project with flair and valued offering themselves to others.

As Jane and her husband attended to the funeral arrangements, it was only natural that the family members began showing up at her house to talk and prepare for the funeral ahead. At the same time, Jane was bombarded with e-mails, texts, and Facebook messages from friends and coworkers who wanted to connect with her upon hearing the sad news. Jane tried to attend to the people in her house, and at the same time, she kept running to the computer to reply and to her phone to answer texts. It left her exhausted and, ironically, disconnected.

When she realized how much the demands of an online community were impinging on her ability to be present with herself and the actual people in her house, she turned off her computer and allowed the e-mails to pile up. She decided to deal with them at a later date.

When Moses was called by God to ascend Mount Sinai, God said to Moses, "Come up to me on the mountain and be there."[15] A Jewish mystic asks, "If Moses had come up the mountain, why did

God also have to tell him to be there? It is possible to expend great effort in climbing a mountain, even to stand before God, but still not be there!" If Moses could stand in front of God and fail to be present, we can physically stand in the midst of family during our darkest hours and yet be somewhere else entirely.

In the weeks that followed, Jane realized that as much as she prided herself in checking off the tasks of her to-do list, she needed to let go of the online demands in order to be present with what was happening in real time. It was her turn to stand on top of the mountain and *be there*—to be present to her darkness, her grief, the loved ones around her, and the work of mourning.

Voiding the Void

People are uncomfortable with, if not outright paralyzed by, the fear of death. When we're uncomfortable, we try to make the discomfort disappear. Well-intentioned family members and friends are often among the first to pull us toward the void dance after the loss of a loved one.

I have seen the slippery slope of trivial words crumble into the void dance at the funeral itself of all places. When friends and acquaintances trickle into the funeral chapel and wait for the grieving family members, who are in a separate room, finishing prefuneral rituals or gathering as a family, the funeral crowd will grow noisier. In this case, I have to step up to the microphone before the family's entrance. I will attempt to restore a natural silence that supports the family in its grief and is a respectful response to the deceased.

I used to shush the attendees, but I came to understand that the noise is a collective response to the discomfort of sitting within the emotional dark, regardless of how many lights are actually on. I learned from a colleague a beautiful lesson that I saw transform a noisy void dance into a venue of support and respect. As she ascended to the podium, she said, "Friends, thank you for being here in support of the family in this time of great distress. Your presence brings comfort to them as they make this journey into and through their grief. When you are quiet and contemplative, your serenity brings a sense of peace to their turmoil and broken hearts. The Jewish tradition teaches that the soul of the deceased is in a state of agitation, a grieving of sorts, because it, too, is on a journey. It is trying to separate from the body and its earthly home. As you are quiet and calm, directing loving thoughts to Samuel, you bring peace to his soul. You are supporting his spirit as he makes his way to the world beyond and as his family makes its journey into the dark unknown. Thank you for fulfilling this sacred role in silence. Your presence and participation are appreciated."

The void dance stops, the community is brought back to the work at hand, and feelings of poignancy and purpose are restored.

I have also witnessed how a condolence call following a funeral can become a dance to sweep the darkness away. This is why, in a traditional shiva home, the rule is that the mourners sit. They must stop moving physically if they are to find an entry into their emotional grief. As they stop, we stop. It's also customary for the mourner to not be spoken to, only sat with, until he or she is ready to initiate conversation. In our discomfort with death and not knowing how to fix things, we try to talk the darkness away. It's too easy to use words to dance around the void. Those who comfort the mourners during a shiva call—a visit to a Jewish house of mourning, a wake, or another venue—need to be conscious and work through their own discomfort around death. If they engage in behaviors that encourage the void dance or inhibit the grieving process, they do a disservice to everyone. We may not intend this, but trivial conversations that divert from the reality of death can quickly turn a house of mourning into a partylike atmosphere. Soon everyone is avoiding the real reason that they are there.

Another transformation of space took place at the shiva home of Charlotte. When Charlotte's mother died, she, her husband, and her children found the first night of *sitting shiva*—opening their home for people to offer condolences and pay their respects—difficult, but not for the reasons one would expect. The visitors were talking, eating, laughing, and catching up about their vacations, work, and children. Charlotte felt as though she was hosting a graduation or engagement party. She felt obligated to resupply the food and the drinks and make sure that everyone had what they needed.

After everyone left, Charlotte and her family had a long talk. Her children were tearful. "No one was even talking about Nana. It was like they were just here for a good time." She and her husband felt the same way. That night, she wrote a list of instructions for those visiting the family during the remaining six nights of shiva. She set the instructions on a table along with the memorial candle and a picture of her mother. The guidelines read as follows:

Thank you for your sympathy during this time of our loss. As we sit together to honor the memory of Harriet Goodman, we ask these things of you:

- Please enter quietly.
- If you have brought food or drink, please put it in the kitchen and tend to any preparations needed.
- If you see any food or drink that needs to be restocked, please help the family by attending to those tasks. If there are tasks that need to be done in the kitchen, your help is appreciated.
- We welcome you to sit with us in silence, if that's what feels comfortable to you, or in conversation as it pertains to our beloved Harriet. We welcome the memories, stories, photos, and thoughts you'd like to share about your time with Harriet.
- Feel free to spend as little or as much time as you'd like in our home.
- We thank you for being with us as we sit in sadness of our loss and in gratitude for the blessed memory and life of Harriet Goodman.

Too Much Too Soon

One of the most common (and perhaps hardest to define) void dances is returning prematurely to regular routines. A thousand years ago, even a hundred years ago, a seven-day pause for mourning was a natural event. This is far from the case in today's world.

Unless you live in an insular enclave, it's difficult, if not impossible, to stave off your responsibilities for long. There's a carpool to drive, errands to run, and work obligations to fulfill. Family, friends, communities, and colleagues should be understanding, but it doesn't always work that way. In a need-it-yesterday society, it's difficult to take the time for the priority of today. No matter how serious you are about facing the void, the world tries to pull you back in prematurely, and you can find yourself doing the void dance.

In the book *I Wasn't Ready to Say Good-Bye: Surviving, Coping, and Healing after the Sudden Death of a Loved One,* the authors share the following about rushing through grief:

> In *Time Wars,* Jeremy Rifkin notes how in 1927 Emily Post reported that a widow's formal mourning period was three years. Twenty-three years later, Rifkin found this period had declined to six months. By 1972, Amy Vanderbilt advised the bereaved to "pursue, or try to pursue, a usual social course within a week or so after a funeral." We impose time limits and expectations for how long one must suffer. While over 90 percent of American companies grant official time off for bereavement, most have established three days as the formal bereavement period for a death within your immediate family.[16]

While family, friends, colleagues, and acquaintances may be well intentioned, too often they encourage mourners to get back to their routines and may rush them to activities too quickly.

Maureen, a seventy-eight-year-old widow, told me that when her husband died two years ago, she listened to the advice of her friends and kept busy. She rushed back to her bridge game and her volunteer work. She accepted the invitations that her friends insisted would be good for her, including dinners out, shopping excursions, and mah-jongg. Family and friends repeatedly told her how wonderfully she was doing. She came to my office on the two-year anniversary of her husband's death and confided that she was exhausted. "I heeded the advice of everyone and rushed back too quickly. I guess in some ways I was trying to be so busy that there wouldn't be enough room to let the grief in." She began sobbing, releasing the emotion that she had worked so hard to keep at bay. My job was to provide the space she needed to express what she had been holding in without moving to fix it. She left that day feeling purged and heard.

Later that week, Maureen opened her husband's closet for the first time since his death and touched all his clothes. She sat on the closet floor and wept some more, and over the next few weeks, she cleaned out his closet. She gave herself the time she needed to touch the heart of her grief.

People who have lost loved ones pressure themselves to reenter their routines prematurely. Even with the best of intentions, the slippery slope of rushing to do "just this one thing" can result in the next dance step of spinning right around the void. One fast errand turns into an afternoon of errands. A quick stop in the office turns into a day at the office, returning a flood of e-mails and calls and scheduling meetings for the rest of the week. An intended quiet Saturday evening having dinner with friends can become a night of too much frivolity and festivities. While you hadn't planned for it, it feels difficult to leave the evening behind. One errand, one meeting, or one outing leads to another, and before you know it, you have returned to your responsibilities and the daily routines of life.

There's nothing wrong with reclaiming those routines. They are there waiting for us, and to find our way back is an important goal. Although the time frame is different for everyone, finding a way back to life prematurely has consequences. The void can't be danced around. It must be danced through, and that takes effort, commitment, and time.

4

RIGHT INTO THE DARK

More important than the quest for certainty is the quest for clarity.

—Francois Gautier

Recently I spent time in the Negev desert in Israel. I stayed in a plush, brightly lit hotel, a juxtaposition against the blackened, cold nights of the harsh desert. It was no surprise when, one night, I ventured out into the desert and couldn't see two feet in front of me. I can't remember the last time I experienced such darkness. However, my eyes began to adjust, and eventually, with the merest sliver of the moon, I could see clearly. Without a flashlight or any artificial light source, I began to find my way along the desert path.

Clarity Right in the Dark

So, too, it is with the darkness that descends after a death. After we settle in, we slowly begin to see. We can't see our ways out of the darkness yet, but we need to take one small, gentle step at a time, even though we aren't sure where we're headed. All we have to do is gain the clarity of a foothold.

Dennis Prager is a nationally syndicated radio-talk-show host, columnist, and social, political, and religious commentator. He has shared on many occasions that he prefers "clarity over agreement." I would modify this to say that I prefer "clarity over comfort." This idea has shaped my understanding of life's darkest moments, and I have come to believe that human beings can endure almost any form of suffering when they have clarity. Having witnessed suicide twice, I can't subscribe to the notion that God only gives us what we can handle. For my grandmother and father, this wasn't the case. For most of us, we can get through our darkest days if we have clarity. We must have clarity to understand what we're enduring, to see precisely what we're up against, and to envision just enough to get through the moment. From that step, we will find another and another after that. We don't have to have a darkness exit strategy. We just have to have a foothold's worth of clarity.

Naming Right into the Dark

The first human act in the Torah is seeking clarity. When Adam sets forth in the Garden of Eden, the first thing he does is name the animals. Naming is an act of power. It's a way of understanding and clarifying what we're facing, and it's the first step in surviving and transcending the darkness. This is why when someone turns to me for guidance through the darkness, my starting point is naming. Each experience with the darkness is unique. When people name and describe the elements in their darkness they find pockets of visibility and light. They begin to transform their wanderings into journeying to find sparks of light.

Joel, a congregant at my synagogue, was able to find a greater sense of comfort and hope as he began naming his darkness. He was married for sixty years and was heartbroken when his wife,

Deborah, died of a stroke. His grief manifested in every pore of his body. He was perpetually hunched over and barely able to acknowledge those around him. Months passed, but he continued to isolate himself and find no relief to his sorrow. His daughter, Irene, called and asked me if I might speak with him.

After I invited him to meet with me numerous times, he finally agreed to come to my office. I tried to get him to talk about his life, children, and grandchildren—anything to begin the conversation. His grief was impenetrable; he responded with one-word answers, and the conversation went nowhere. I asked him to tell me about the darkness and to try to name it. I told him he could give me one-word descriptions, nothing fancy, just whatever came to mind. He started slowly. "Agonizing. Horrific. Scary," he said. Eventually his words morphed into sentences, paragraphs, poetic soliloquies, and heartbreaking diatribes. He looked up at me startled, yet relieved, for having purged himself of the intensely painful feelings that he hadn't articulated even to himself.

As he settled into the idea of naming his darkness, he shared his fears of being unable to get by in life without his beloved Deborah. She was the heart and connector in the family. Would he know how to relate to his family and friends without her at his side? He told me that he was fearful of the silence when he woke up in the morning and when he went to bed at night. He wondered who could he talk to now that she was gone and who would be there for him now that he was alone. He was fearful of learning to do the things that she had done for him, such as grocery shopping, cooking, and arranging their activities.

Over the next few weeks, as Joel continued naming his fear of remaining adrift and isolated, we talked about how he could deal with those fears one step at a time. We talked about his children and grandchildren who were eager to have him back in their lives. We talked about taking a cooking class at the senior center. I explained that he wouldn't only learn to cook, but it would get him out of the house and engaged with people. It was the beginning point of identifying where he was in the darkness and a path toward the light.

Naming the darkness gives you a starting point. This allows you to figure out where you are and what you're facing so you can begin to walk through it. In the words of the Swiss psychiatrist Carl Jung, "One does not become enlightened by imagining figures of light but by making the darkness conscious." In naming the darkness, we restore within ourselves a sense of power. When death's darkness descends, we're stripped of both our loved ones and sense of control. When we name the darkness, we reclaim fragments of who we are, what we are, what we have, and what we truly own. These are the sparks within the darkness waiting to be discovered. With each word we speak, we give voice to our experiences. With each conversation about suffering, terror, and despair, we chip away at death's dark grip. Naming, locating, describing, and ultimately owning our pain is the first step in shifting from wandering to journeying. As our eyes adjust, we continue to move forward.

While Joel named his darkness to understand what was holding him back and what would help him return to life, Sue learned to name her darkness to understand what would help her prepare for her death. Sue was in her sixties when she came to me to talk about her terminal illness. She was understandably distraught, but she hadn't shared the news with anyone, not even her children or grandchildren. She broke down, crying out that she was afraid to die and afraid to tell anyone of her impending death. For her, nothing we spoke about or discovered in our conversation would change the fact of her illness, but clarity allowed her to navigate through the darkness with purpose and meaning.

We gain clarity by confronting the darkness and articulating our feelings about it. This opens our minds and our hearts. We gain clarity by having people around us who allow us to articulate this truth and allow us to be honest and real. As we open up, we find something solid to stand upon—one idea, one belief, or one truth. From there, we put one foot in front of the other and make the journey into the unknown.

Sue pushed forward and began talking about the dizzying darkness that swirled about her. She began to say that she wasn't nearly as afraid of dying as she thought. She was afraid to die, but what she feared even more was leaving her children and grandchildren behind. She was devastated that they wouldn't have a mom or a nana to witness their milestones, celebrate their joyous occasions, and share their lives.

Her children and grandchildren were her foundation, her truth, and her touchstone. As she articulated this, her darkness began to give way. I could see it in her body language and in her ideas. As we continued talking, we came upon an idea. She would dedicate the time she had left to archiving her life and leaving what we called a "library of blessings."

Sue videotaped herself talking to her children and grandchildren at different stages of their lives. For her unmarried daughter, she recorded a wedding blessing; for her infant grandson, a bar mitzvah blessing; for her son, a midlife transition blessing; and on it went. She made audio recordings of blessings and wrote letters of blessing to be opened on birthdays. She transformed her darkness into something meaningful and profound for herself and those she loved. In some ways she defied death. In the words of Edgar Allan Poe, "The boundaries that divide life from death are, at best, shadowy and vague. Who shall say where the one ends and where the other begins?"

Sue's words, spirit, and love live on in the hearts of her loved ones and in the legacy of blessings she left for her family's future. She transformed her wandering into a journey. In so doing, she bestowed upon her children and grandchildren a sense of clarity that would help them on their own journeys through the darkness. She gave them a gift in her life and in her death.

Right into Anger and the Dark

Another way we gain clarity and enter into the darkness of our grief is by being honest about what we're feeling. So often when helping guide people through their grief, I see mourners desperate to fight the truth. They avoid telling the truth about their feelings to me, and they often fail to tell the truth to themselves. There's a Jewish proverb that asks, "What is truer than the truth? The story." The stories we tell ourselves about our lives, our relationships, and our feelings become our truths. It's crucial that we learn to be honest about what we feel after a loss. The darkness can be dispelled only with honesty and clarity. When it comes to emotions like love, it's easier to be honest. When it comes to darker emotions such as anger, half-truths or outright lies begin to take root.

We live in a world that is often uncomfortable about emotions, particularly darker ones like anger. Anger is typically viewed as a negative and the opposite of kindness or love. Emotions are neither good nor bad. They are what they are, and they serve different purposes. Anger can be an important emotion that guides us through the darkness, even though at first it can feel endless. Anger is the second stage of Kubler-Ross's five stages of grief, and despite being afraid of its strength, the more you're able to experience the anger, the more it will dissipate and lead to healing. Anger is often the most loving response. We rebuke our children out of compassion and concern, not malice. When we feel anger toward people we love—especially when our loved ones have left us, even if not of their own choosing—the response is natural. The Dalai Lama, one of the most celebrated teachers of peace, remarked, "Generally speaking, if a person never shows anger, I think something's wrong."

When Noah came to me, he was in his late twenties. He had two young children, and his wife, Mary, was dying of late-stage cancer. He wasn't seeking me out because he was heartbroken, to deal with his sadness, he felt he could go to family, friends, or almost anyone. But Noah was angry and felt he had nowhere to turn to express these feelings. Noah was furious and had no shortage of reasons why he felt that way. He was angry with God for "giving his wife cancer." He was angry with the oncologist for not curing Mary's cancer and with her primary physician for not detecting it earlier. He was angry with her parents for not being more financially supportive because he'd had to quit his job to tend to Mary and the kids. He was mad with their friends for not being more present during the treatments. He was mad with the senior rabbi of the synagogue where I was working for not visiting Mary in the hospital more often.

Most of all, he was angry that no one would allow him to vent his anger. He felt like everywhere he went, he was forced to pack it up and put it away. He felt like everyone made him feel as if his anger was wrong and needed to be reined in. He felt like people thought he was a bad person for being angry, particularly because he was most angry with his wife.

Noah loved Mary dearly, and that was why he was so angry with her. He was angry that she had not done breast examinations early enough to find the cancer. He was angry that she turned to alternative healers when she was diagnosed. He was angry that she didn't have disability insurance and that she hadn't signed them up for a premium medical-insurance plan—their funds for the mounting medical bills were running out. He was angry that in the prime of his earning potential, he'd had to leave his job to take care of her and the kids. Most of all, he was angry with her for dying. It wasn't supposed to end up this way. He needed his wife, and his kids needed their mom.

During our sessions over the next few months, Noah vented his anger. He came to discover, as he ranted in the safety of my office, that he wasn't as mad as he was scared. He wasn't as angry as he was sad, and he wasn't as much fuming as he was grieving. He needed a safe place to go and a person to listen to him, and then he was able to move through his anger, be present with his wife, and share their final days together in honest, real love.

The anger that may arise within the darkness shouldn't be brushed under the carpet; it can be helpful to find meaning and hope and to lift the layers of pain that are underneath. There are many expressions of anger that mourners might experience as they confront their grief, and in the process, they can gain insight into their deepest concerns.

They might be angry with God for allowing death to take a loved one. They might be angry at the injustice of life for taking their beloved and not someone else. They may be angry with the dead for not having taken better care of themselves, heeding the doctor's advice, or going to get checkups as requested. They may be angry with loved ones for killing themselves. They might be angry at the unfinished business in a loved one's life and the dreams they had of being with him or her cut short.

Perhaps they are angry for the way the person left things before dying, not having done this or prepared that or having said this or left that unsaid. Maybe they're mad at themselves for what they did or didn't do or for saying what they said or for what they failed to say.

Whatever the source of the anger as they face the darkness, by admitting that there's anger in that space, they give anger its due and validate its importance. Anger means that something real is at work.

In the words of Elie Wiesel, a Holocaust survivor, author, speaker, and Nobel Peace prize recipient, "The opposite of love is not hate; it's indifference. The opposite of art is not ugliness; it's indifference. The opposite of faith is not heresy; it's indifference. And the opposite of life is not death; it's indifference."[17]

Even if our loved ones are no more, the feelings we have, including anger, remind us that we're far from indifferent, and they tell us that the relationships continue. Instead of eliminating anger, we're well served to heed the advice of the Koretzer Rabbi: "I conquered my anger long ago and placed it in my pocket. This way I don't allow it to consume me, and if I need it, I take it out." There are times to put your anger away. There are other times (such as righteous indignation, if that helps to reframe it) when it's important to take out your anger and experience it.

Experiencing anger isn't the same as acting out in anger. Whether siblings or entire branches of a family refuse to talk with one another during normal times is one thing, but boycotting a funeral or house of mourning or fighting with family or fellow mourners when the darkness descends is something else entirely. It adds to the darkness and prevents us from grieving.

Anger and Families Right in the Dark

Although there's no such thing as a dysfunctional family—because there's no such a thing as a functional family—when death's darkness sets in, some function well under stress. In other families, the dysfunction grows. Perhaps sadder than families rushing back to their busy lives and not sitting long enough together in the dark are the families that refuse to sit together at all or sit together and need to be pried apart.

I have seen this anger rip through families. It ranges from passive bickering to physical fights. There are disputes between siblings, parents, children, or the extended family around every end-of-life issue imaginable. Did Dad want a Do Not Resuscitate (DNR) order even though he never wrote it down or mentioned it? One sibling insists yes, and the other says no. While a mother is struggling to take her last breaths, siblings are fighting over who is entitled to which valuable item. Long-standing hostilities between certain family members can become exacerbated through the dying process, the funeral, and beyond. One person refuses to go to the condolence meal at a particular venue, while another is adamant about denying a family member's speaking at the funeral. There can be disputes over finances, legalities, inheritances, and logistics. In the mourning period, and sometimes for years, decades, or the rest of their lives, families can turn on one another. This casts an additional darkness that is a tragedy unto itself.

Nothing good comes from prolonged family disputes, exiling, snubbing, or disrespect. It doesn't serve the memory of the loved one or the lives of the mourners. No matter how substantial the issue being argued, it's another way to dance around the void. The strategies, calculations, manipulations, and rehashed dramas are distractions that take the bereaved away from the issue at hand. The longer they live within the distractions, the longer they push off entering their grief and moving toward healing.

Family drama is nothing new. Dysfunctional families are as old as the Hebrew Bible, and within it, there's story after story of family strife. Abraham is estranged from his son Isaac. Brothers Isaac and Ishmael are distant as a result of the dynamics of their parents' relationship. Isaac's sons, Jacob and Esau, are at one another's throats, and Joseph's brothers, due to their jealousy, throw him in a pit and tell their father, Jacob, that Joseph is dead. The combinations of family *mishagas* (craziness) are endless. The stories are there to put our own family dysfunction into perspective. In almost all of the stories, as turbulent or hate filled as the family might have been, the death of a parent served as a time of unification rather than division because matriarchs and patriarchs would rise to the occasion.

If only that were true today. A while back, I officiated at the funeral of the Smith family. The patriarch, Mr. Smith, had died. The elderly Mrs. Smith confided in me how terrified she was of facing the loss of her husband and the funeral. The Smiths had three daughters, two of whom had not spoken to each other in years. No one could remember what caused the latest breakdown, but this was one of many during a lifetime of disagreement and distrust. They refused to see or speak to one another. Mrs. Smith obsessed over whether or not her daughters would show up for the funeral. Her fear was palpable, and she recounted how horrible it was that her husband couldn't have all his girls at his bedside when he was dying to bless them and be blessed by them as he left this world.

True to form, two of the daughters refused to be together at any family function, including the funeral and the shiva. Their heels were dug in, and nothing that anyone said could change their minds. The funeral proceeded with two of the three daughters in attendance. No matter how meaningful it was, it was still shrouded in unnecessary darkness. The family had experienced a tragedy in losing a beloved husband and father. Sadly, the tragedy was compounded because two grown women were committed to their anger. Until they find a path of reconciliation, they will continue to wander in the darkness.

There's a time and place for anger, and it often serves as a catalyst to help us fix what is broken. We need anger to overcome injustice, to right our wrongs, and to make sure that we learn from the past. The dark is rife with emotions, and whatever we're feeling, including anger, is what we should be feeling. The work of the dark is first to clarify the emotion. What is the anger about? Can it be used to make necessary changes, or will it continue to fester and lead to destruction? Once we clarify what it is, we can use the emotions rather than be used by them. They help us harness our energies for the mourning process. With each moment of honesty about our emotions and with every attempt at truth about where we are, another spark is discovered, and a little more darkness is dispelled.

Clarity Right in the Midst of Dark Confessions

Mourners often pull me aside at the hospital as their loved one is dying, at the funeral home as we prepare for the service, or at the mourners' home after the burial. They ask, "Rabbi, does it make me a terrible person that I'm relieved my father is dead?"

One woman felt guilty about the relief. She had been dealing with her father's illness logistically and emotionally for years, and she was exhausted. A man had been angry with his father for his whole life, and with his father's death, he was both relieved and consumed with guilt.

Jill came to me for counseling months after her mother died, and she was still wracked with guilt. Her mother's death was difficult enough, but what was tearing Jill apart was that her mother had had severe Alzheimer's disease during the final few years of her life. Because Jill was an only child, it was left to her to tend to her mother while she was alive and to take care of the funeral arrangements after had she died. Jill was a dutiful daughter, but she was beating herself up over the fact that in the final months of her mother's life, she had stopped visiting her on a regular basis, and at the end, she barely saw her at all.

"I couldn't take it anymore," Jill said, sobbing and wiping her nose with tissues. "I would visit my mom, but she usually didn't know who I was. It was so painful and distressing not only to be unrecognized but also to endure her verbal abuse. She was angry and mean—so different from the woman she had once been. I felt as if my mom was already dead, and this was an impostor in her body. When she died, I was relieved. Am I a horrible daughter? Am I a horrible person?"

I asked, "Did you provide a safe, caring facility for her to live in?"

Jill nodded through her tears. "I got her into the finest Alzheimer's unit in the area."

"Did you check in with her caregivers periodically to see how she was doing?"

"Absolutely, all the time."

"Did you treat her with dignity the times that you did visit?"

"Of course."

"Then you have nothing to feel guilty about. You did nothing wrong."

"But I hated that woman in the Alzheimer's unit. I was grateful when she died. How can you say that I was a good daughter? How can I be a good person?"

My response to both Jill and anyone who has acted in a similar way and expressed similar feelings is the same: as important as your feelings are to you, and as much as you need to work through the anger, guilt, indifference, or anything in between, they're not the central issue. Feelings are real in that they have an impact on the person experiencing them, but they don't have a direct impact on the world. It's wonderful for someone to have positive feelings accompany his or her positive actions, but we aren't entirely responsible for our emotions. We're responsible for our behaviors. We can't be tried for murder for thinking about killing someone. We can't be guilty of adultery for having a fantasy of infidelity, and we can't be judged for our thoughts about a loved one.

If you spend years tending to an ailing mother, feel ready for her to die, and even wish she would die so that you can get on with your life, it doesn't make you a bad person or have any impact on her death. It makes you human. Experiencing anger toward a father after he takes his life doesn't make you a bad son. It makes you real. Feelings need to be recognized, understood, and dealt with, but you aren't judged for having those feelings. The commandment doesn't say, "Love your mother and father." It commands us to honor them. Honor isn't a set of feelings. Feelings can't be commanded, but actions can, and honor is within your control.

Relationships are complex and messy. They are often filled with betrayal, abuse, neglect, tragedy, and darkness. We shouldn't judge ourselves for what we have wished for, consciously or unconsciously, or the emotions that may have surfaced. We should honestly reflect upon how we acted or didn't act in the face of those feelings. Did we serve our loved ones in life and in death? This isn't to ask if we served them *perfectly* with some prescribed notion of doing things in a perfectly loving way. Did we give of ourselves the best we were able? We're human and imperfect, and at times, we all grope within the dark.

It's important to take stock of your finer moments and strengths as well as the times you were unable or unwilling to step up to the task.

Regret, guilt, and disappointment are important steps on the journey through the darkness, and they help us evolve. To categorically write off our shortcomings isn't the answer when moving through grief.

Be honest with yourself about your efforts and actions. It's the only way that you can learn to do better and give more. It's the only way that you can forgive those you've lost for what they did or didn't do for you; it's the only way to forgive yourself for what you did or didn't do for them.

In the words of the philosopher Kierkegaard, "Life must be lived forward but can only be understood backward." It's crucial that we look back at what was but, at the same time, not beat ourselves up for what we did or didn't do. In the journey through the darkness, we must be honest about what we think and truthful about what we feel. With each courageous encounter, we discover greater clarity.

The Right to Cry into the Darkness

When dealing with the darkness, shedding tears is one of the most clarifying of all human experiences. Tears are one of the most interesting, powerful, and complex expressions of emotion. They are uniquely human, and the act of crying is profound. As a Native American proverb goes, "The soul would have no rainbow if the eyes had no tears." The tears we cry for emotional reasons have a different chemical composition than tears shed for other reasons—tears of sorrow have significantly greater levels of protein than tears that result from an eye irritant.[18] While we may not fully understand the significance of the hormonal properties of this type of tear, we know that crying out of sorrow can be an enormous physical and emotional release.

The poet and philosopher Samuel Taylor Coleridge wrote the following:

A grief without a pang, void, dark and drear,
a drowsy, stifled, unimpassioned grief,

which finds no natural outlet or relief,
in word, or sigh, or tear.[19]

We're moved by tears. The tears of a baby move us to take action. Watching a loved one, or even a stranger, cry moves us to empathy and compassion. I was sitting in a Starbucks, and a woman burst into a torrential downpour of sorrowful tears. Suffice it to say that the café stopped, and all attention was redirected toward this woman. Businessmen, nannies, children, and the delivery guy stopped in their tracks. There was a genuine outpouring of sympathy from people who were, seconds before, strangers. There's something powerful, mysterious, and holy in tears.

We're often so uncomfortable with tears that we quickly wipe them away. In their book *On Grief and Grieving: Finding the Meaning of Grief through the Five Stages of Loss*, Elisabeth Kubler-Ross and David Kessler illustrate this point with the following story:

> A mother survived two of her three children. When the first one, a son, died, she was so overcome by grief she fell on the casket and cried out loud. Her husband gently pulled her to her feet, and the funeral continued. When her second child died, her own mother took her grieving daughter aside before the funeral and said, "Don't make a scene like you did last time. The tears will ruin your makeup. Do you have any idea how your face looked the last time with mascara running down your chin?"
>
> She faced her mother and said, calmly, "Do you have any idea what will be ruined if I don't cry?"[20]

The authors explain that in their grief groups, there's a rule that everyone has to grab their own tissues. Sometimes when a person starts to cry, others grab the tissue box and shove tissues at them. While this may be a compassionate response, it often sends the message, "Hurry up and stop crying." As we move into the role of caretaker, we avoid our own darkness if we rush to pat dry the evidence of sorrow.

Tears are divine. The Jewish mystic Rebbe Nachman said, "My tears are my divinity; they come from the inside of God's face."

As those who have had a deep, authentic soul cry know, it's nothing less than full attention to something that demands to be poured out. When we're in the role of supporting mourners, we have a duty not to rush to stop their tears with our words or to push tissues into their hands. We must sit with them as witness to the grief they are bearing. When we're mourning, we should remember that to have a soul cry is to enter the darkness of our lives, relinquish control, open ourselves up, and offer every ounce of thought, emotion, and spirit to the broken places. Through exposing those broken places, we understand the lay of the land of our brokenness and see how to move through the dark.

After the initial shock and waves of emotion when my father died, I struggled the most with the fact I couldn't cry. Even after the funeral, I was unable to shed a single tear. I went to the synagogue to say Kaddish, the Jewish mourner's prayer, for him, but my eyes remained dry. I wrote about him every day during the weeks after his death, and still there were no tears.

One day while I was jogging, the floodgates opened. I couldn't cry while praying, writing, or talking about him, but I could cry on the running trail while my body was moving and my endorphins were pumping. For whatever physiological or esoteric reason, the tears flowed. In time, the tears stopped. The grief was released, in no small measure, thanks to the gift of movement. Over the years, writing has offered me clarity of mind. It has been crucial to map where I've come from, what I'm dealing with, and where I'm headed. However, body movement, particularly yoga and running, offers me clarity of emotion. The term *emotion* speaks to this idea of feelings in motion. Through writing, I think differently, but through physical movement, I feel differently. Each activity is an essential component of clarity as I find my way through the dark.

I can't tell you how many people have approached me after I tell this story to share experiences of their own. They relate grieving encounters they have had while dancing, biking, or walking along the beach. They express great relief because they carried feelings of guilt, failure, or inauthenticity at not connecting to traditional modes of mourning, what they believed was the right way to grieve or the proper time for tears.

Sometimes tears come through verbal prayer or body movement. Sometimes they come when we hear particular songs or pass particular sights or when we're alone in silence. Sometimes the tears flow in profound moments, family gatherings, life-cycle events, or anniversaries. At other times, they come during trivial moments such as a sappy commercial, a silly song, or a random comment. Many mourners find that the tears come when they are alone in their cars.

Whenever they come and whatever the reason they are triggered, tears are a gift that should be greeted with appreciation, not held back or quickly wiped away. They express something that words can't convey. Just as we must learn to enter the dark in the service of healing, so must we learn that releasing emotion, as painful as it might be, is the process of sorrow working through us.

As we open up, let go, and release the sorrow beyond speech, we feel the words of the psalmist when he wrote, "Tears may linger for the night, but joy comes with the dawn."[21]

5

RITES WITHIN THE DARK

*We do spiritual ceremonies as human beings in order to cre-
ate a safe resting place for our most complicated feelings of joy
or trauma so that we don't have to haul those feelings around
with us forever, weighing us down.*
— Elizabeth Gilbert, author of *Eat, Pray, Love*

I n my home, we speak with our children about "special time."
For my kids, it's something that approaches heaven. We create moments of "special time" by going on outings, doing fun
things, and sharing time together in special ways. In my family,
"special time" is the ultimate reward.

The Rite Way Home

When my father died, as painful as the time was, being with
family after the funeral at the shiva home was a new way for me
to think about "special time." I assumed that *special* meant *happy*.

However, being with family and friends—some of whom I hadn't seen in decades—listening to stories about my father, and watching my kids spend time with their cousins was special. Although it was far from happy, there was a joyousness in spite of the circumstances. I kept thinking how proud my father would have been if he had seen the response to his life and his family's closeness during our bereavement.

This is one reason why it's painful to see modern families rewrite mourning rituals or eliminate them altogether. Many rituals have been refined over millennia for the sole purpose of guiding us into the darkness. These rituals are effective only if we partake. Otherwise, we end up like Joe.

Joe and his dad were close, and the whole family was tight-knit. After a beautiful and fitting funeral for his father, everyone was baffled by Joe's decision to call off the shiva. He did the perfunctory condolence meal, but by the end of the day, before the market closed, he was back at work. The rest of the family was caught off guard. They had assumed they'd be sitting shiva for a couple of days, or even a week; however, no amount of reasoning or guilt could deter Joe. Although the family sat shiva, without the newly appointed patriarch at the helm, the house of mourning felt doubly empty.

I hardly knew Joe, but my experience in subsequent counseling sessions confirmed what I had suspected. Contrary to what others in the community were saying about his behavior—that he was cold, callous, or cruel—I saw that this wasn't the case. Joe was heartbroken and petrified. He couldn't begin to imagine facing life without his father. He was scared to become the patriarch of his family and show his emotions in front of his family, friends, and community. He did what he had done when he was a little boy and afraid of the dark: he ran and hid. He shared with me that when he was a kid and something was bothering him, he hid in his tree house or immersed himself in sports.

The grown-up Joe was still scared, but his fears were now bigger and more complicated. He was still hiding. It wasn't in a tree house or in playing sports; it was in his office under a desk load of work. He was terrified to stare into the void and face the dark.

This is reminiscent of the story of Adam and Eve in the Garden of Eden. After they eat the forbidden fruit and discover their nakedness, they run and hide, unable to stand exposed in vulnerability and shame. God's question to them isn't one of accusation but one of invitation. *"Ayekha?"* (Where are you?)

I asked Joe this question. Part of the work of facing his fears was to return to these questions: Where are you? Can you remain within the storm of grief and stand there with an open heart?

Just as Adam and Eve had one another, Joe had others who were ready to sit with him and be with him. Equally important, others were waiting to help him face the darkness that was descending upon the family. Until he faced the rawness of his grief, his family couldn't confront its own. Joe needed to meet the darkness, stop running, and return home. Through sitting in the darkness with family and friends, our eyes eventually adjust, and sparks of light begin to emerge.

Last Rites: The Power of Funerals and Rituals

I have seen the power of a funeral as a clarifying force many times. Every society, culture, and religion has end-of-life ceremonies. It's remarkable that even today, in a world that has pushed away so much of what traditional religions offer, almost everyone has a funeral that is religious or spiritual in orientation. There's good reason for the universal nature of religious rites and funerals in particular—they work.

Though I'm liberal when it comes to religious rituals, I'm a traditionalist on issues surrounding death and grieving. It doesn't matter to me what religion we subscribe to or traditions we turn to; all that matters is that in those moments, we have something larger than ourselves to turn to for guidance. When death's darkness descends, I encourage mourners to default to those traditions rather than forego them or modify them to the point that they lose their power. The traditions have withstood the test of time. Often tradition needs to be modernized, but when it comes to mourning rituals, more often than not, the traditions work to help set the stage for the process of grieving to unfold by physically releasing the body and emotionally concretizing the grief by publically demonstrating that life must go on without loved ones present in this world.

Marcus was a happy, and seemingly healthy, four-year-old when he had a seizure. When he was medevacked to the nearest hospital, tragedy struck. As the helicopter ascended, an undiagnosed brain tumor and the pressure of ascending in the helicopter killed him instantly. His death could have been averted if he had been driven by ambulance. It was an unimaginable horror, and his family and community were devastated.

One of the complications surrounding Marcus's death was that his family, living at the time in Boston, was British, and they wanted the burial in England. However, because of the complications of his death, pending investigation, lawsuits, and complexities of transporting a body overseas, even under the best of circumstances, it would be weeks before Marcus was laid to rest. His family needed something in the interim, so we planned a memorial service. It was the most painfully beautiful service I have ever conducted or witnessed. On the one hand, it gave the family and community an opportunity to stop and process their grief. On the other hand, it would be weeks before they could finish dealing with the myriad details surrounding his death. In addition to the hell of losing a son so tragically, they were caught in a mourner's purgatory, far from the light of life but also unable to immerse themselves in the darkness of death. They couldn't begin to move forward until their boy's body was returned to the ground.

On many occasions, I have seen a family forced to delay a funeral. For days—and in rare instances, weeks—the family, friends, and community are in limbo until the body is returned to its final state through cremation or burial. Not coincidentally, the first human in the Torah is called *Adam* because he's taken from the *adama*, or ground. Physically, and perhaps metaphysically, we need our loved ones to be returned to the earth or scattered to the winds before we can orient ourselves.

When the Greenbergs came to me, having just lost "Bubbe," their mother and grandmother, they asked if I would officiate a private graveside service. They weren't interested in the rituals leading up to or following the funeral, and the funeral itself was to be "short and sweet." They said, "Rabbi, we want it to be meaningful but minimal rituals and prayers. Moving, but no eulogies."

I said that I would respect their wishes, and there's a time and place for doing less, but I sensed this wasn't one of those times. It felt forced, as if it was masking something else. I had been a rabbi long enough to know that as harried as we are in our day-to-day lives, in the aftermath of loss, if we're rushing or skipping rites and rituals, we're probably void dancing.

After a bit of gentle pushing, what I suspected was confirmed. It wasn't that they wanted to get the ritual over with and get on with their lives. Bubbe was the matriarch of their family, the end of an era, and they were caught off guard with her death and unprepared to deal with all it entailed. There were condos on the East Coast and West Coast to pack, cars to sell, lawyers to deal with, and many other tasks. It wasn't that they wanted to rush through the funeral nearly as much as they felt rushed by the onslaught of all that awaited them. They were inundated by their sorrow and darkness.

I assured them that, like many others who had to face loss, everything they had to deal with would be tended to in time. However, this moment, right now, was one they would never be able to get back. I told them that I had never met a family that regretted doing more rather than less in regard to the rituals of death, but I had known many families that felt incomplete or regretful for not doing as much as they could have at the time.

The Greenbergs heeded my advice, had a full chapel service with speakers and eulogies, and then sat shiva. They took care of their grief and fully mourned Bubbe. They were grateful and unified as a family, and in time, they took care of the condos, the cars, and the other loose ends.

Funerals provide the sacred space to move those in grief down the path of mourning. While *grief* and *mourning* are often used interchangeably, there are important distinctions between them. Grief is the emotional reaction and response to loss, while mourning is the process we go through in connection to the loss and in acclimating to living without a loved one physically present. The funeral is an important intersection for the bereaved to begin expressing grief as they begin the mourning period. When people don't have a funeral, or when it's significantly limited, this has the potential to create suffering.

A few years back, I met with fourteen-year-old Jason. Every year, he counted the days until overnight camp began. He was away at summer camp when his grandmother died, and his parents decided not to tell him about her death. She lived across the country, and the funeral would have entailed a long flight, necessitating a big trip for Jason in the midst of his favorite time of the year. His parents figured they were doing the right thing by letting him enjoy his summer without having to bear the burden of the loss. They reasoned that there would be enough time once camp was over to talk to him about his grandmother.

They had made an appointment for me to speak to Jason. Ever since learning about his grandmother's death two months prior, he'd been withdrawn. He begged to quit his soccer team and didn't want to invite his friends over anymore. When they asked him what was wrong, he told them he was fine, went up to his room, and shut the door. They weren't sure what to do, and they thought he might open up to me. The last time I had talked to Jason was the previous year when he prepared for and then celebrated his bar mitzvah.

When he walked into my office, I was amazed at both his growth spurt and the way his shoulders tensed and his head hung down. It was almost as if he were trying to grow back inside of himself. I reminisced about his bar mitzvah with him and then asked him to tell me what stood out about that time for him. He mentioned that it was the second-to-last time he had seen his grandmother. I asked him to tell me more about his grandmother and watched as he tried to blink back the tears. He said that he was mad at his mom and dad for not telling him that she had died. He was angry that he wasn't given the choice to attend her funeral and felt that they had treated him like a child by making the decision for him. More than anything, he had a hard time believing that she was dead because he wasn't there for any of it. He didn't know when it happened, and he never got to be part of the funeral experience. He didn't see the physical expression of death or see his grandmother be buried. He asked, "What if I was clowning around with my bunkmates or playing capture the flag while she was being buried?"

I have seen how a funeral can help individuals and families find their way through the maze of darkness. When people don't know where to go, where to be, or what they should be doing, rituals and ceremonies help bring the frantic period to a close. The time to reflect on their loved ones is crucial while moving toward the funeral.

It's partly for this reason that in Judaism, and other faiths such as Islam, the body is returned to the earth as quickly as possible. From the religious perspective, this is so that the soul can find closure from this world and begin its ascent to the world to come. It's equally for the mourners so that they can begin their descents into the darkness. A funeral, a memorial service, a celebration of life, or another type of gathering is a way of consciously allowing the phases of mourning to unfold.

The funeral helps us transition from the abstract, chaotic realm of the surreal to the concrete, disciplined realm of the real. The service gives voice to the deceased, the individual mourners, the family as a unit, and the community. A meaningful funeral helps the mourners to stop and reflect, and it allows the family to embrace, reminisce, and pay proper tribute to the deceased. It's an opportunity for friends and community to support those in mourning. It provides a role for all of those gathering within this symphony to honor death and celebrate life.

Parents often ask me what to do about their children (about eight years old or younger) in regard to funerals. Children can generally handle much more than we give them credit for, and they are more comfortable with death than we realize. Much of the discomfort is the parents,' not the child's. It's like most anything else in life. If we believe something, our children will believe it. If we're scared or doing the void dance, it will trickle down to them.

Sometimes the decision of whether to allow younger children to attend a funeral is secondary to how the decision is made or communicated. Like adults, children need clear communication about what has happened, regardless of whether or not they attend the funeral or burial. If they are old enough to love, they are old enough to grieve. They need the truth about the darkness in shades that are appropriate for their ages.

The Rite to Speak: The Rite to Listen

Funerals are centered on eulogies and stories about our loved ones' lives. "Days are like scrolls," writes the medieval rabbi Bachya Ibn Pakuda. "We write on them what you want remembered." A funeral is a time to take out the scrolls of someone's life and read from them. This collective sharing gets to the heart of the Native American saying, "It takes a thousand voices to tell a single story." Through the stories and reflections that are shared, a collective clarity emerges.

I've heard it said that a person dies two deaths: one when the body dies and the other when the person's story dies. The essence of a eulogy is to put a voice to the darkness. In his book *Sum: Forty Tales from the Afterlives*, neuroscientist David Eagleman says, "There are three deaths. The first is when the body ceases to function. The second is when the body is consigned to the grave. The third is that moment, sometime in the future, when your name is spoken for the last time."[22] As we move through the darkness, one of the greatest sources of light comes when we see that part of our sacred duty is to learn our loved ones' stories, record them, and recite them. A good eulogy is a starting point in this process because it can be both clarifying and profound. It's sublime when it works.

Sometimes funerals and eulogies fail to bring clarity and comfort; they can muddy the waters of grief and add to stress. Some mourners find clarity and comfort in writing and delivering their loved ones' eulogies. For others, it's more helpful to forego the stressful act of public speaking and sit and listen to the clergy or others share their stories. Sometimes this decision is an easy one to make, but at other times, stressful dynamics are played out. I've watched siblings argue for hours because two out of three want to give the eulogy, and then the third is pressured into speaking as well. Sometimes a family member will be forced to stand up with the other family members despite his or her pleas to sit with the other mourners. I've watched parents push children to speak at the funerals of dead grandparents despite the children's insistence that they're terrified of doing so. Some parents have gone so far as to proofread, rewrite, or write the eulogy that they think is best for their children to read about Grandma or Grandpa, regardless of what the children want.

These scenarios beg the question of whose needs are being served and what is underneath these expectations. When people are forced to speak or speak on a whim, the mourners rarely experience the grief of their losses because their attentions are pulled to the uncomfortable scene unfolding at the pulpit. In my experience, thoughtfully exploring who would like to speak or not speak and why allows for authentic expression. The speaker and the listener are both active participants, and both are necessary to allow for the full weight of the experience. I'm reminded of words from Shakespeare's *Macbeth*: "Give sorrow words. The grief that does not speak whispers the o'er-fraught heart and bids it break."

The person giving the eulogy speaks on behalf of the mourners, giving voice to their losses as a whole. The modern word used for magical incantation, *abracadabra*, is an ancient Aramaic phrase. The original, *avrah k'dabrah,* means, "I will create as I speak." As the casket is lowered into the grave, as death's darkness descends on the mourners, the family, and the community, death is met actively, not passively. The funeral, the eulogy, the words, the cries, and the screams remind the mourners that we aren't without power. The funeral and all its details need to be thought out and thoughtful but not held too tightly. There are no *shoulds, musts,* or *have tos.* There's no such thing as perfection. Asking for perfection at the funeral is asking for the darkness to be prematurely diminished or airbrushed to a glossy finish. Neither gets to the core of the complex expressions of a grieving heart. Funerals, eulogies, rituals, and rites are human responses to suffering. They are our attempts to address the unanswerable and endure what might otherwise be unbearable. The right ritual makes room for the darkness. The best rites take us farther down the path and help us give voice to our grief, yet as it's said, the darkest hour is just before the dawn.

6

THE DARK NIGHT
OF THE SOUL

One may not reach the dawn save by the path of the night.
—Kahlil Gibran

The year was 2007. My father seemed to be rebuilding his life, and the darkest days appeared to be behind him. He had a new wife and a new community. That is why what happened next was all the more shocking.

My Darkest Night

On an ordinary fall morning, my dad drove to a sporting-goods store and bought a rope, a seemingly ordinary purchase to the guy behind the counter. He returned home, knowing that his wife was out. He sat at the kitchen table and wrote a brief letter plus a short memo on a sticky note. He walked up the stairs to his bedroom, took the rope, and attached one end to an exposed beam above his bed. He placed the letter on the bureau and posted the note on the door. The sticky note read, "Do not enter. Call the police." He stripped himself of his jewelry, tied a slipknot, and placed the rope around his neck. He stepped up onto the bed and stepped off this mortal plane. He died with his feet a few inches above the ground. His monsters had won. Instead of climbing through and over his mountain of grief, he fell headlong into the void.

The day of my father's death, my stepmother called me at the office to tell me of the tragedy. At the time, I was out, so my assistant took the call. My stepmother informed her as to why she was calling. My assistant shared the tragic news with the cantor—the synagogue leader who sings or chants liturgical music for the congregation—who happened to be both my colleague as well as my childhood cantor. He knew my father and had been friends with my grandfather, as well as officiated at my grandmother's funeral. In many ways it was almost divinely appointed that he would be the one to deliver the tragic news to me. As I returned to the synagogue, the cantor, with a grave look upon his face, took me into the sanctuary away from everyone else. There he held me squarely by the shoulders and as gently as possible said, "Baruch, your father is dead. He took his life just a few hours ago." I think he kept talking, but that was the last thing I heard. All I remember was pummeling the pumpkins and squash that were on the stage, as it was the holiday of Sukkot—a Jewish festival of the harvest—and above all else, I remember screams, and realizing that the screams were coming from me. Perhaps it was learned. Perhaps it was primal. Perhaps it was my ancestral call, but for the second and—God willing—last time in my life I heard those horrendous and pleading words, "Why? Why? Why?" that my father had cried out to me after his mother had killed herself, and this time they were emanating from me.

As horrible as hearing the news of my father's death was, the nightmare was magnified in the days following it. I became obsessed with the need to understand not only why he took his life but how he did so. Perhaps it was morbid curiosity or a form of avoidance, or maybe I intuited that until I filled in some of the blanks and gained some degree of clarity, I could never anchor my darkness or heal.

I began to research methods by which people took their lives. What I discovered horrified me. I learned that my father probably did not die quickly. Death by hanging can be instantaneous if your neck breaks. If it does not, as was the case with my father, you can hang for minutes before you die. I thought of my beloved father hanging there with time to realize what he had done. I wondered what he was thinking before he went unconscious. Was he thinking of my siblings and me? Did his grandchildren cross his mind? What if he regretted his choice and wanted to undo what he had set in motion but was helpless to do so? I found out that most suicidal thoughts come and go within five seconds, so most suicide attempts go unheeded. What if on the sixth second he had changed his mind?

It kept me awake at night. I agonized as I tossed and turned, wondering why he did it and what he was feeling as he left this world.

I returned to his home and the scene of this nightmare. My only request during the visit was to be given time alone in his bedroom where he spent his final moments on earth. I was surprised at my need for the details. Many people said to me, "What's the point? Let it go. The details don't matter." To me, the details mattered tremendously, and as I discovered while guiding others through grief, I'm not alone in the need for what others might find futile details.

I sifted through his sweaters, trying to hold on to his distinct scent. I retraced his footsteps to where he took off his ring. I put his ring on and took it off, trying to imagine what it must have felt like for him to place his ring there while knowing it was the last time he would do so. He couldn't have known that I would pick that ring up, put it on, and never take it off. I sat on his bed, imagining him tying a slipknot, the kind he had taught me when I was a Cub Scout. I lay back on his bed, clutching his pillow in despair and disbelief—a few days prior, my dad had been lying in that spot, calculating his exit strategy from life. I found myself staring up at the beam he had chosen, and I noticed a groove in the wood that looked peculiar. It dawned on me that this scar was created by the rope and the weight of his body as he hung from the beam. *What if the rope had broken? What if the beam had been too weak and split in two? What if I had walked in and had been able to save him?* The what-ifs bombarded me as I lay there.

I moved from what-ifs to bargaining—*If my dad can only live again, I will spend my life doing only good works*—to avoidance—*If I close my eyes and refuse to see the beam, can I wake up from this nightmare?*—to anger—*Only twelve inches away from the bed, couldn't he have reached his leg out and pulled himself back?*—to the unanswerable question: *How could he do this to himself? To us?*

As my mind spun, another painful realization dawned on me. From what the police report said, it became clear that the position in which my father died put him directly facing the bathroom mirror. *What if my father's final seconds were spent staring in the mirror? What if his reflection was the last thing he saw, and what if he regretted what he had done? What if my poor, wretched father died having to bear witness to this atrocious end?* This was the what-if that broke my heart. Like a stormy sea smashing against the rocks, these thoughts kept coming at me and pounded me deeper into the depths of darkness.

Rock Bottom

The nature of darkness is that it's unknown, and we fear that there will be no way to climb out and into the light. In twelve-step recovery programs, there's an understanding that until someone hits "rock bottom"—the depths of suffering—recovery is rarely possible.

Hitting rock bottom doesn't imply that people can't sink further. Rather, it implies a degree of exasperation and an unwillingness to continue on the descent. It represents a willingness to stop the free fall and bring the darkness to an end. It's the realization that there's too much at stake and that they will risk everything and everyone in their lives if they continue downward. Rock bottom is about resolving to begin the long, slow march to the surface. It reminds me of the words of Jung: "When you are up against a wall, be still, and put down roots like a tree until clarity comes from deeper sources to see over that wall."

Though I remained at rock bottom for some time, trying to absorb the pain and get my bearings, I stopped the free fall and began to put down roots. Ironically, I discovered that at rock bottom, a newfound sense of purpose grew in me, not in spite of my father's tragedy but because of it. "The Serenity Prayer," written by theologian Reinhold Niebuhr and adopted by Alcoholics Anonymous (AA), speaks of the recovery from that dark place and a new understanding of it: "God, grant me the serenity to accept the things I cannot change, the courage to change the things I can, and the wisdom to know the difference."

I was a long way off from internalizing these words, but I knew that finding my way out of the dark would require focusing on what was within my power to change.

We read in the Psalms, "The Lord is your shade."[23] The Jewish mystics interpret this as meaning that God isn't merely your shade; God is in your shade, your shadows, and your darkness. The darkness isn't devoid of God. It's often where God is most profoundly felt. Sometimes we have to hit rock bottom to fully experience God or be ready to meet God. Maybe it has nothing to do with God per se; maybe the darkness is where we meet our true, authentic selves.

The Dark Night of the Soul

Examples of rock bottom or "the dark night of the soul," as it's often called in spiritual circles, abound. The phrase comes from a poem written by Saint John of the Cross in 1578 while he was imprisoned for being an advocate of church reform. He narrates a dark journey of the soul that descends in pain until it hits rock bottom. This journey through the darkness is a sort of purification. Only when the soul can fall no further does it begin its ascent to light, love, and life.

Throughout religious traditions, there's a motif of great men and women, mystics, and heroes making the journey from darkness to light. For many, the dark night of the soul precedes a renewed sense of purpose and vision.

Joseph Campbell, the foremost thinker and author on the nature and power of myth, describes mythical heroes and the journeys they make. The heroic journey entails obstacles and challenges that ultimately lead to transformation and a return to life's light. During this journey, there's a dark night of the soul, or what Campbell calls "the ordeal." The ordeal is the *nadir*, the low point along the hero's path when she or he has descended to the depths of despair in confronting tragedy or death. Every mythical hero descends into the darkness and eventually ascends out of it into a new life. In the words of Ernest Becker, in his Pulitzer Prize–winning book *The Denial of Death*, "Heroism is first and foremost a reflex of the terror of death. We admire most the courage to face death."[24] The hero is born within the ordeal, and there's no greater ordeal than facing death. This is why the great figures of various faith traditions experience this dark night of the soul and enter their ordeals alone.

Moses enters deep despair on multiple occasions. He hits rock bottom when God punishes him for his disobedience, and the consequence is that he will never enter the Promised Land. Not coincidentally, this punishment comes after the loss of his beloved sister, Miriam. As the Israelites are complaining about a lack of water, Moses is so busy tending to them that he fails to tend to his own grief. In a fit of despair, he loses his temper, defies God, verbally accosts those he's leading, and lashes out in anger. This isn't a story about a leader who disobeys God as much as it is about a man who leaves his darkness unattended. As a result, he flounders within the dark.

Moses is revered through the ages because he picks himself up and rises from this low point with new certainty and grace. Eventually, he will look out over a land that he will never enter. He knows that his darkness had purpose and his suffering helped him ascend. His legacy will be carried by those who enter the Promised Land. They will carry his story forward and share it for generations to come.

In his final hours on the cross, Jesus cried out in pain and fear, "My God, my God, why have you forsaken me?"[25] These are words uttered in despair as Jesus faced the physical and spiritual trials of his crucifixion for the benefit of his purpose. Through his suffering, he moved from the darkness to the light with his final words, "Father, into your hands I commit my spirit."[26] Amid his doubt, he moved through darkness and transcended it, arriving at a place of faith, certainty, and light.

Prince Siddhartha left the extravagance of his palace to discover truth and reach enlightenment. His search brought him to five ascetic monks who practiced extreme austerity as a method of finding inner peace. Siddhartha practiced with his companions in this way for six years, ceaselessly seeking a way to conquer the body in order to reach the soul. In forsaking worldly pleasures like those he had known at the palace, he practiced starvation and self-mortification. Far from moving him toward enlightenment, these actions brought physical and emotional darkness. Emaciated and near death, he collapsed in a river while bathing and nearly drowned.

A girl named Sujata was passing by and saw the weak man who looked more like a corpse than a living human being. She knelt beside him and offered him rice pudding, which he received with gratitude. As he let himself become physically nourished, he realized that a life of self-indulgence was no better than a life of self-annihilation. He sat under a bohdi tree and vowed not to get up until he discovered the truth of life. After forty-nine days, he attained enlightenment, and became known as The Buddha, meaning, "one who is awake." He formulated the Middle Way that encompasses the Four Noble Truths and the Eightfold Path. Through his darkness, he discovered the light within and taught his followers that we all have an inner light that can guide us from darkness. He taught the importance of self-trust and inner wisdom, and in the Mahaparinibbana Sutta he urges each person should be a lamp unto yourself.

Rebbe Nachman of Bratzlav, known to his followers as Reb Nachman, was the great grandson of the founder of the Chassidic (Jewish mystical) movement. He was a renowned leader and mystic in his own right, and he struggled mightily with depression. Nachman's work was heavily impacted by his depression, which he referred to as his "bitter darkness." Much of his teaching revolved around working with this bitter darkness, not allowing it to overwhelm him, and offering hope and inspiration to a multitude of followers.

Nachman had a revolutionary notion of the Israelite exodus and the nature of slavery. To him, slavery was being bound by emotional or spiritual shackles rather than physical ones. For him, there was no greater spiritual shackle than the bitter darkness. When we're within that darkness, we struggle to experience the light of the divine or light of any kind. We struggle to move toward the promised land that holds the gift of light and love. Nachman's life was dedicated to exemplifying that light can be found within the darkness and that it's our duty to find a way to turn our darkness into light. It wasn't in spite of his darkness that he transformed the Jewish world, inspiring a resurgence of spirituality and joyous ecstasy in the tradition, but because of it. Within that bitter darkness, he discovered and shared the sweetest light.

A 2007 book entitled *Mother Teresa: Come Be My Light* reveals a woman who spent decades being terrified in her darkness of doubt.

In 1959, Mother Teresa wrote, "In my soul, I feel just that terrible pain of loss, of God not wanting me—of God not being, of God not existing."[27] According to the authors, this inner turmoil, known at the time by only her closest colleagues, lasted until her death in 1997. Even with the darkness that surrounded her, she found holy sparks that lit an entire world.

Jung said, "As far as we can discern, the sole purpose of human existence is to kindle a light in the darkness of mere being." Great men and women throughout history have exemplified this. They have gone through the darkness and wrestled within the abyss of doubt, pain, fear, and loss. The dark night of the soul is that place where trials appear, and the choice is whether, in that darkness, we can see the test as a flicker of light that can restore us, illuminate our lives, and benefit others.

There's always a rock bottom as we descend into death's darkness. Some sink for days, while others sink for years. Hitting rock bottom comes in various forms, but in that darkness, there can be a shift that allows us to gain a foothold and find a point from which to begin the ascent. Regardless of the time frame, I have witnessed that something empirically changes about people during this shift. Their outlooks and attitudes change, and even their physical appearances are different after their own dark night of the soul. The Pulitzer Prize–winning poet Mary Oliver said, "Someone I loved once gave me a box of darkness. It took me years to understand that this, too, was a gift." Though the shift is often messy and always painful, it's an essential part of the journey of mourning as we transform from darkness dwellers to seekers of light.

Dark Night: Death of a Child

When Melissa began her freshman year at Cornell University, her parents, Janet and Kevin, worried about how their only child would transition from home to a campus environment. While she called home over the first few weeks with some pangs of homesickness, she quickly fell in love with college life. All summer long she counted the days to return to her dorm, friends, and classes. Waving good-bye to her as they drove away from the campus, they smiled at one another with joy, knowing that she was happy to start her second year.

Three weeks later, they received a call and learned that Melissa had been hit by a car while riding her bicycle home from class. Frantic, they rushed to Ithaca, New York, to be at her bedside. Melissa never regained consciousness, and she died two days later. They were devastated. When they believed that the situation couldn't become worse, they learned that Melissa had been riding her bicycle safely on the sidewalk. The driver was drunk and had veered off of the street.

The loss of a child goes against the natural order of things, and as Melissa's parents watched her coffin being lowered into the ground, they felt like the world had collapsed over them. They wondered how the world could keep on spinning and why they should allow themselves to continue spinning right along. They asked, "Why Melissa?" Their anger at God rivaled their anger at the drunk driver who was responsible for her death. In the aftermath of their loss, they found it impossible to spend time with friends who offered their love and support. They knew that their friends meant well, but it was too hard to be in their presence, knowing that *their* lives were safe and their children were alive. They clung together in their grief, cutting themselves off from family and friends and barely going through the motions of living. They couldn't find a rope to hold on to or an anchor to ground them.

They replayed what would have been her last moments on that bicycle on a beautiful fall day. They tortured themselves with imagining what her future could have been—a career and husband and the grandchildren she would have given them. They avoided the places Melissa used to frequent and the people she spent time with. To put themselves in those situations, her father explained, was like a dagger in his heart. Months later, their doorbell rang, and Melissa's mom opened the door to find Melissa's best friend, Carrie, standing in the doorway. It was winter break, and though Carrie had been hesitant to contact Melissa's parents since the funeral, she felt compelled to visit them, despite the fact she knew they were keeping their distance from family and friends. Carrie collapsed into Janet's arms, and the only thing Janet could do was hold Carrie and sob with her. They went into the house and sat together on the couch.

Hearing the sobs, Kevin rushed down the stairs to see what was happening. A thousand images of Carrie and Melissa over their eighteen-year friendship flashed in front of his eyes. They cried, shared their grief and despair, and shared their stories of Melissa. As the stories were recalled, they laughed in memory of her antics. That was the beginning of release and hope.

Dark Night: Facing Our Mortality

At eighty-five years old, Roger was diagnosed with metastasized lung cancer. He had been suffering from Alzheimer's disease since he turned eighty and had struggled with depression much of his life. While he had enjoyed great success as a businessman, he had forgotten much of his accomplishments due to dementia, and his family tried to remind him of his proud career. After the cancer diagnosis, the family walked on eggshells.

Despite the prognosis that gave him less than six months to live, his wife, Rita, didn't want him to know that he was dying. They were in their own home, and when people from a hospice service visited, she told him that it was a visiting nurse so that they didn't have to drive in the winter to the doctor's office. Roger grew more agitated and increasingly weaker. Sometimes he cried and asked to see his mother, who had died nearly fifty years prior. Many times a day he cried out, "What's wrong with me? Something doesn't feel right."

His daughter, Rachel, came to visit. She insisted that they tell Roger about his diagnosis and the fact he was dying. She held his hand and told him how much she loved him, and she told him that the doctors had discovered that he had lung cancer; that was why he felt so weak and sick. Roger had a look of shock and confusion on his face, and then he asked Rachel to repeat what she had just said. She told him again, and he began crying. After a few minutes, he said he was scared and had known something was wrong with him. He asked how long the doctors thought he had left, and he spoke with a clarity he had not shown in a long time. He talked about his life and said that he wished he had more time. He was understandably sad and scared, and while he had been crying for months, the tears he shed upon hearing the news of his impending death were anchored to a grief he understood.

Rachel called Rita in and explained why telling him, rather than hiding the news, was better for all of them. He deserved to know. There was a moment of tearful hand holding and, even with this dire news, relief.

A few minutes later, Roger asked the same questions he had been asking for months. "What's wrong with me? I don't feel right. I'm scared. What's happening to me?"

It was clear that he had forgotten what they had just discussed. Rachel realized with horror that she was going to have to tell him again about his lung cancer and impending death, and he would have to re-experience learning the horrible news.

For the rest of the day, the three of them relived the darkest of moments as the pattern repeated. Rachel remembered it as if she was falling through an abyss, and just when she thought there was a bottom, she fell again. For Rachel and Rita, retelling and reliving the fact of Roger's dying—and him having to hear it repeatedly—became a living hell.

Over the next two months, the family rarely, if ever, mentioned cancer in front of Roger, and the proverbial elephant in the room weighed on them. It was unclear how much Roger remembered or understood, and so the implicit decision was to avoid the topic of death, which meant that there was no room to say good-byes. Ten weeks after the diagnosis, Roger ended up spending his last days at a hospice house. The doctor told Rita how important it was for her to talk to her husband, even if he couldn't respond, and to say good-bye. Standing at his bedside, Rita and Rachel talked to him as they held his hands. They talked of their love, their cherished memories, their promises to him that they would be OK and that they would remember him and love him always. He squeezed their hands. They arrived at the bottom. In that place were words and gestures of love that helped them move toward the surface of life and light.

Dark Night: Contemplating Suicide

George was a medical researcher who had gained international acclaim for his work. He was divorced and the father of two daughters, aged ten and twelve. He was also an alcoholic and a drug addict. After a police arrest, the partial loss of custody of his children, and revocation of his medical license, he couldn't see a way out. He hit rock bottom.

As he drank gin and sobbed alone in his house, a plan took form. The wild thunderstorm pounding on his window matched the pounding of his heart. He rummaged through his bathroom cabinets and found the combination of pills he needed. He wrote a note for his girls and left it on his kitchen table. He grabbed the bottle of gin, felt for the pills in his pocket, stepped outside, and locked the kitchen door. Rain pelted his face while he headed for the car. He remembered thinking that he could do it there in front of his house, but for some reason, he felt he had to keep moving.

The clock in the car read 10:52 p.m. He started to drive, and the windshield wipers barely kept up with the torrential downpour. He drove south through Connecticut as the radio blasted and the sky cried rain. Something in him pulled to drive farther, to be anonymous in New York City, and to be one more poor soul who ended his life in the crowded streets of strangers.

He pulled into an alley in a grungy neighborhood and glanced at the clock. It was 3:32 a.m., and as he opened his bottle of gin and took a swig, he sobbed, knowing that this night would be his last. He poured the pills into his hand and fortified himself with more drink. As he was about to throw the pills into his mouth, he noticed a piece of paper sticking out of the glove compartment. For some reason, he pulled it out to see what it was. A shock of recognition ran through him as he saw a business card he had stored there. It was the card of a woman he had met months ago. She had written down the information about the AA meetings for doctors that she went to in New York City.

Was that why something in his subconscious had pulled him to drive there on the darkest of nights? Something shifted in him, and he put the bottle of gin under the seat, threw the pills out into the street, and slept until the morning light drifted into the alley. He waited in his car for a bit before driving to his first AA meeting.

The descent toward rock bottom feels like a vast expanse of hopelessness, and it's often when we believe we will succumb that a sliver of light appears. It's up to us to follow that light, search for meaning in our mourning, to cry out, hold on, and eventually, let go.

7

BREAKING DAWN

Not knowing when the dawn will come, I open every door.
—Emily Dickinson

When I sat in my father's bedroom, imagining his last act in life, I screamed into the darkness. I called out to God, and in that act, I heard the echo of my soul. Rumi said, "Cry out! Don't be stolid and silent with your pain. Lament! And let the milk of loving flow into you."

Crying Out, Holding On, and Letting Go

This crying out can take many forms. Sometimes, it's screaming. Other times, it's a painful call of "why me? Why our family?" It may involve a crisis that leads to a reexamination of beliefs, a reprioritizing of values, and a new understanding of our spiritual selves, or it may be discovering how we connect to ourselves, others, and the sacred. In the psalms, we read, "Out of the depths I cried to you, my Lord. God, hear my cry."[28]

When we cry out to God, the divine, a higher power, or the darkness itself, we hear our own voices and our own fears and hopes. We can wake ourselves up and prepare to move toward light and life.

Judith was in her eighties when her only child, Bruce, died after a long struggle with cancer. She had lost her husband a few years prior. During Bruce's dying process, and even at the funeral, I did not see her cry or release much emotion. She was lost in a broken silence.

Upon returning to her home, where she was sitting shiva and receiving visitors, something changed. Judith began crying and then screaming. Nobody knew what to do. Everybody wanted to help her, but she pushed away their attempts to console her. Her sister turned to me, saying, "Rabbi, do something."

I said, "I am doing something. I'm letting Judith scream."

As a therapist friend of mine taught me, "Better out than in." Judith had been holding it in and was now letting it out. Her release of emotion was a sign that she was shifting. She touched rock bottom, and from there, she would begin her ascent again.

In the Jewish mystical tradition, there's a custom during the month preceding the High Holy Days to prepare for the sacred occasion. It continues to this day, particularly in the Israeli city of Tzfat (Safed). Worshippers go into the woods late at night, descend into the riverbeds, and scream, "Abba, Abba," (Father, Father) repeatedly. The High Holy Days are a time to face what we have done or not done, been or not been, or become or not become that has perpetuated darkness in the world. The practice is a way of acknowledging the darkness, being honest about it, and committing to enter it over the course of the month.

To scream into the darkness is to hear what is in our hearts, whether we—or others—want to hear it or not. It often entails a reevaluation of what we once held dear or believed in or the assumptions we have made about life. Often after a death, I'm asked if it was a punishment from God. The mourner will ask, "Did I do something wrong? Did she sin against God? Is this divine retribution?" At other times, I hear someone say that God blessed his or her family by saving a family member from a deadly car crash.

In either case, I invite the conversation of what it means to assume that God would punish one person and save another. I challenge people to look at their beliefs and the ways they influence their behaviors. When there's a cry in the dark, it's important to listen to what the cry is saying. We must determine if it's a cry that will strengthen the person's relationship with him- or herself, others, and the sacred or if the cry will weaken those connections. Kubler-Ross says the following:

> True spirituality is not about blaming or finding fault. It's about reaching into the purest part of yourself, the part that is connected to love, the part that is (if you believe it to be) connected to God, the part that is beyond the body and health and disease.[29]

When we cry out, it's important first to hear the cries and then to determine what cry will move us toward a place of light, love, hope, and possibility.

As painful as it is, hitting rock bottom represents a shift. It's the moment of possibility and hope that the suffering can be transformed into meaning and growth. Pliny the Elder, the first-century Roman philosopher, said, "The depths of darkness to which you can descend and still live is an exact measure of the height at which you can aspire to reach." The darkest hours after we lose loved ones aren't without opportunity. The further we delve into that darkness, the higher we can ascend into the light.

Susan, a woman in her midfifties, was devastated when she lost her husband, Stan, to brain cancer. She was a devout Christian, and he was a less-than-observant Jew. As long as I had known them, Susan had practiced her religion fully and, at the same time, was in many ways was more engaged in Judaism than Stan. This was why it was so striking after he died to see her renounce her faith, as well as her ties to all organized religion. The last words I heard from her, shortly after the funeral, had to do with her feelings that religion was full of childish beliefs and that she couldn't believe in a God who would allow her husband to die such a tragic and painful death. Her religious foundation crumbled beneath her, and over the next few months, she plummeted into a pit of doubt and despair. She was done with God.

We lost touch for a while, but a few years later, she made an appointment to see me. She shared that after those dark days of grief, she began to rebuild her life with religion at the center. Her faith became so pivotal to her climb out of the darkness that she found her way to the seminary and became a Unitarian minister. She said, "It wasn't that I didn't believe in God after Stan died. I was so angry, confused, and hurt that it clouded my spirit, but what I discovered through those long, dark, lonely nights, where I felt nothing but pain and had nothing but tears was that I wasn't alone. I felt that God was with me. Stan was dead—I understood that—but I was alive. The best thing I could do, both for myself and for the blessed memory of Stan, was to reach out to life." In her ministry, Susan has a gift for sitting with others during their most challenging times because she has touched the darkest place in herself and learned where to seek the sparks of life.

Along with crying out during the dark night of the soul is the act of holding on. Harriet Beecher Stowe, the American abolitionist and author, said, "When you get into a tight place and everything goes against you till it seems as though you could not hang on a minute longer, never give up then, for that is just the place and time that the tide will turn." Picture a ship sailing in the midst of a mighty storm. The huge waves are roaring, and the sea is churning. Thunderbolts crash, and lightening streaks across the darkened sky, making the passengers on the boat shudder. The possibility of capsizing becomes a reality. Those on the ship must hunker down and find a mast or something they can anchor themselves to as the wind rushes and the waves crash.

It was during such a violent storm that the British sailor and slave trader John Newton found hope. Though he had lived a life of darkness and had contemplated both murder and suicide, he cried out to God for mercy in what was to be his spiritual encounter. He transformed his darkness into light, left the slave trade, studied Christian theology, and became a prominent abolitionist. He also became an Anglican clergyman and wrote the famous hymn "Amazing Grace." These words have inspired countless people lost in the dark:

> Amazing grace, how sweet the sound,
> That saved a wretch like me.
> I once was lost but now am found,
> Was blind, but now I see.

In our grief, we're like those passengers on the ship, and the depths of our despair threaten to overwhelm us. It feels like we might drown in the ocean of mourning, so we focus on breathing— one more inhalation and exhalation. We hold on tightly through the darkness. When the storm feels less threatening, or we find those things that can serve as our life vests, we need to let go. We need to let go physically and metaphorically lest we remain frozen in fear, unable to move forward.

In the words of Andre Gide, winner of the Nobel Prize for literature, "One doesn't discover new lands without consenting to lose sight of the shore for a very long time." One moment at a time, we test our strength in the ocean of grief as we search for support and solid ground. We have to learn to let go of what was to arrive at what could be.

Rumi said, "Life is a balance of holding on and letting go." It's an art to know when to hold on, and equally so when to let go. When what you held on to for support is holding you unnecessarily in one place, it's time to let go. Anchors can help you hold on during the storms, but they also prohibit you from setting sail to new lands.

The Narrow Bridge

Rebbe Nachman, who spent a lifetime battling life's darkness, grappled with the notion of holding on and letting go. He summed it up in his maxim, "The entire world is a very narrow bridge." Life is a narrow bridge that is suspended between two tenuous poles of life and death. Beneath us lurks the dark chasm of doubt and fear. When those who walked beside us are no longer there, we touch the fragility of our steps upon that bridge and are fearful of walking forward. Nachman understood that to be frozen in our tracks is that same as being frozen in our lives. The darkness can never be defied by sitting in it indefinitely, and the way to move through it is to walk that narrow bridge through the darkness. This is why his saying ended with these words: "The world is a narrow bridge, but the essence is not to let fear keep you from crossing." He reminds us that fear must not be the defining hallmark of our lives.

In *The Denial of Death,* Ernest Becker says the following:

> The fear of death must be present behind all our normal functioning in order for the organism to be armed toward self-preservation. But the fear of death cannot be present constantly in one's mental functioning else the organism could not function.[30]

While we must be aware of the bridge that spans life and death, we must let go of fear so that we can live more fully.

Nachman's statement about life as a narrow bridge draws heavily from the Hebrew Bible, rephrasing perhaps the most well-known verse: "Yea, though I walk through the valley of the shadow of death, I will fear no evil, for you are with me."[31] The verse is among the most often used in funeral liturgy. It's so popular that, regardless of religion or lack of religion, many know it by heart. We know it because we know that it cuts straight to the heart of death's darkness. We also know that we must journey onward. After loss, deep within the valley of the shadow of death, we must make our ways through that valley and across that bridge, placing one foot in front of the other. As AA teaches those rising from the depths, we must take it one day at a time.

Limping to the Light

The matriarchs and patriarchs of the Bible were humans with strengths and weaknesses just like you and me. What made them great wasn't perfection. Rather, they had a resiliency of spirit, a relentless drive, and a quest to pick themselves up off rock bottom and set forth across their narrow bridges. Each one faced the darkness many times in myriad ways.

Jacob faced the dark repeatedly and painfully. The grandson of Abraham and Sarah was so deeply defined by the darkness that nearly every one of his God encounters took place in the dark. Every time was a struggle and, often, a brutal one. Jacob carried with him a tremendous weight of regret, loss, and grief. Until he confronted his darkness, he couldn't know the light of day. Eventually he hit his rock bottom.

> And he took them and sent them over the stream and sent over that which he had. And Jacob was left alone; and there wrestled a man with him until the breaking of the day. And when he saw that he prevailed not against him, he touched the hollow of his thigh; and the hollow of Jacob's thigh was

strained as he wrestled with him. And he said: "Let me go for the day is breaking." And he said: "I will not let you go until you bless me." And he said unto him: "What is your name?" And he said: "Jacob." And he said: "Your name shall no longer be called Jacob, but Israel for you hast wrestled with God and with men and have prevailed." And Jacob asked him: "Tell me, I beg you, your name." And he said: "Why is it that you ask about my name?" And he blessed him there. And Jacob called the name of the place Peniel: "for I have seen God face-to-face, and my life is preserved." And the sun rose over him as he passed over Peniel, and he limped on his thigh.[32]

Was Jacob wrestling an angel? Was it a man? Was it his brother, Esau, from whom he had been estranged? Was it God? Was it himself? The only thing that is clear is that Jacob confronted something painful and profound. He confronted not merely the darkness of night but his own dark night of the soul. Within that darkness, he was transformed. As dark gave way to light, his name was changed from Jacob to Israel, reflecting this transformation. In Hebrew, the name Jacob comes from the root word *ekev,* which means "heel," which referred to his birth when he held onto the heel of his brother. As he wrestled, he had to let go in order to receive the blessing for which he yearned. In that moment, his name was changed to Israel, which means "one who struggles with God and man and prevails."

Within the darkest aspects of our lives, the potential for growth exists in the struggle itself. In Hebrew, the modern word used for crisis is *mashber.* It derives from the root *shavar,* meaning "to break," but it can also refer to a beginning. In the book of Isaiah, the word *mashber* refers to the exit from the uterus, and in the Talmud, *mashber* stands for the bed or chair on which a mother gives birth. Where there's crisis, there's opportunity. Endings bring with them beginnings, and death is often accompanied by birth. Jacob's dark night of the soul is painful and terrifying, yet within this crisis, he's reborn into the light of day.

When we wrestle with our fears and demons and struggle with life after the death of loved ones, we can undergo transformation and move forward. Like Jacob, we will have battle scars, and they will stay with us indefinitely. We read, "And the sun rose upon him...and he limped upon his thigh." Jacob's wounds may heal, but they also reflect what he has undergone. With a transformed name comes a transformed gait; Jacob walks with a limp for the rest of his days. We can find the sparks of light and life as we move forward, but we're changed by our ordeals. Like Jacob, the battles we face leave us both transformed and scarred.

Jacob was transformed through this brutal ordeal, but he's the one who did the transforming. At his rock bottom, he made a decision to take back his power from the darkness. "I will not let you go until you bless me," he said to the darkness. That is to say, "I will not accept this as meaningless. I will not rest until this moment yields blessing. I will not stop seeking until I discover sparks of light." It's only then that the light of day shone upon him—limp, scars, wounds, and all.

This was Jacob's task, and it's our task as mourners. As we move through the depths of darkness, we will be able to move forward authentically—scarred and limping but with breathtaking beauty because of the truths we have learned. Writer Anne Lamott states the following:

> You will lose someone you can't live without, and your heart will be badly broken, and the bad news is that you never completely get over the loss of your beloved. But this is also the good news. They live forever in your broken heart that doesn't seal back up. And you come through. It's like having a broken leg that never heals perfectly—that still hurts when the weather gets cold, but you learn to dance with a limp.[33]

Our scars tell the stories of our loves, our losses, and our deepest yearnings. They are testaments to the battles we have faced, the tenacity we have demonstrated, and the miracle that we have survived. David Richo, a psychotherapist and writer, states, "Our wounds are often the openings into the best and most beautiful part of us."[34] Our wounds aren't things to be hidden away. On the contrary, our scars are what make us beautiful. They are what make us real.

Years ago, I met a woman named Maxine at a yoga studio. I knew that she was special but couldn't articulate why. She was probably in her seventies, and at one time, she must have been beautiful. But the years had been hard on her. She had many wrinkles, and in some places, they were almost deep fissures carved into her face. Her once-black hair was dry and silver. Although she did yoga every day, she was hunched over and appeared frail, almost brittle, as if time had weathered her.

Even still, something about Maxine fascinated me. Maybe it was the fact she was the only yogi in the studio who was over the age of forty. Maybe it was that she looked so different from most of her contemporaries—no hair dye, no makeup, and definitely no Botox injections. Whatever it was, she had an air of regality and an aura of power in spite of her frail body. I wanted to know what it was.

After I attended this class for more than a year, we bumped into each other at a local café and sat down for a chat. It changed not only the way I thought of Maxine but also the way I thought of physical beauty, particularly the lines we have on our faces. Over the next few hours, she shared with me what anyone would deem a tale of woe.

Maxine grew up in a world of privilege. She was wealthy and beautiful. She married a successful businessman and had a beautiful daughter, and then everything changed. Her daughter died in a car crash, and her life fell apart. Her husband left her for another woman and, in the process, left her nearly destitute. About ten years after that, she was diagnosed with breast cancer.

Maxine's life would have brought most of us to our knees, and yet our conversation that day wasn't a tale of woe. I left the café feeling inspired. During our talk, she shared with me the depths of suffering she had endured, but she had met every tragedy head on. After each battle, she mourned, healed, and moved forward in her life.

Although we hardly talked after that encounter, other than the usual pleasantries when we passed in the yoga studio, from that day on, Maxine captivated my heart. I saw her silver hair as a lion's mane. Watching her in the warrior pose, I understood how she lived as a warrior. Above all else, when I looked at her face, I no longer saw wrinkles. I saw warrior marks, and I have referred to them as such ever since. Every line on her face told a line of her story. Every crevice was a test endured and a testament to a battle she had faced down and won. Maxine was radiant and glorious. She taught me that warrior marks are stripes to be earned, lines to be won. She taught me that battle scars aren't to be hidden away but to be displayed proudly. The world can see the realness of who she is and what she had endured through her warrior marks.

Journeying through the dark valleys and across the terrifying bridges will necessarily entail wounds. These wounds are central to our mission. They become part of the past that will inform our futures. They aren't to be hidden away or looked on with pity. They serve as reminders that we have touched the darkest corners and are still journeying forward, moving toward the light.

Being Real

Perhaps you remember *The Velveteen Rabbit*, by Margery Williams. It tells of a toy rabbit's quest to become loved and to become real. Along his journey, the title rabbit meets the Skin Horse, and the following conversation ensues:

"Real isn't how you are made," said the Skin Horse... "Generally, by the time you are real, most of your hair has been loved off, and your eyes drop out and you get loose in the joints and very shabby. But these things don't matter at all, because once you are real you can't be ugly, except to people who don't understand.[35]

Darkness isn't an end but a beginning. Within darkness, we're conceived and birthed. According to both the Bible and the big bang theory, before there was light, there was dark. The Torah describes this primordial state as a deep, chaotic, dark emptiness. In a sense, this dark emptiness is a womb in which life gestated. Whether for the origin of the universe or an embryo in its mother's womb, darkness is the incubator of life. Darkness may be the absence of light, but it isn't empty. The sparks of possibility and life-giving attributes are waiting to be discovered within it.

8

SPARK SEEKERS

It is better to light a candle than to curse the darkness.
—Chinese Proverb

The journey we make after the deaths of loved ones must begin in the dark. In Ecclesiastes, we read, "There is a time for everything and a season for every activity under the heavens: a time to be born and a time to die...a time to weep and a time to laugh, a time to mourn and a time to dance."[36] We have a need to know what time it is within our lives and to enter it fully, regardless of how others react. Wandering into the darkness is an essential step through the seasons of grieving, but it can't be the last step. Just as there's a time for death's darkness, there's a time to rise from that darkness and journey into the next season.

Rising from the Dark

In the Jewish tradition, when the sun has risen on the seventh and final day of shiva, we leave the darkness and journey back toward the light. The mourners, aided by family and friends, leave their houses for the first time after a week and walk around the block. This ritualizes the end of this stage of the mourning process. This doesn't mean that they are done with their grief; it means they are committed to returning to the daily rhythms of life. The mourners may not be ready to let go of some of the darkness, but the tradition pushes them to take that next step, regardless of their feelings.

At some point, you have to get up, get dressed, and attend to the obligations of life. Sometimes the journey has to be willed into reality, and you have to go through the motions in spite of what you feel. In the words of motivational speaker and best-selling author Tony Robbins, "Emotion is created by motion."[37] Leaving the darkness behind may entail going through the motions that ultimately carry you out into life. When the darkness beckons us to stay frozen beyond its appointed season, we must rise up from it, whether we're ready or not.

Fake It till You Make It

When I met Donna, she was a young mother with two girls, one in preschool and the other in elementary school. Her husband was killed in a car crash, and upon hearing the devastating news, our community came to a halt. Fellow preschool parents took care of her children, and congregants and community members cooked and cleaned for her. Her mother flew in from out of town to take care of her. For nearly two months, everyone rallied around her to help her and her daughters get through the terrible time.

After a couple months, everyone had to return to their own busy lives. Even though they were ready to move on, Donna was still deep in the darkness of her grief, but her life couldn't remain in a holding pattern. The season was shifting, and Donna, against every fiber of her being, had to lift her head off her pillow, rise out of her bed, and get back to her duties as a mom. There were school lunches to prepare and a carpool to drive. She had to sell her home and begin looking for a job. She did what she had to do as she went through the motions, but she confided in me that she felt like a fraud.

She said, "Rabbi, all I want to do is to curl up in a ball and hide in my bed. I'm doing what needs to be done, but I feel like a fake. People ask me, 'How are you doing?' but they are just being polite. They don't want to hear the truth anymore. I tell them I'm OK, but what I want to tell them is the truth. I'm *not* OK. I force myself to smile in front of my girls, and I hold back my tears. My pantry has become my secret crying place. I continue to pretend. What choice do I have? It's awful, this play acting, pretending that I'm OK when I feel horrible."

I shared with her a teaching by Nachman: "Even if you don't feel happy, you can fake it. Pretend to be happy." We agreed that faking happiness isn't an aspiration, but sometimes, in order to move forward, it can help.

Donna jokingly said that her new mantra was, "Fake it till you make it."

She kept faking it, but for the next year, she was far from making it. But she went through the motions of her new normal life and eventually found that she was no longer faking it. One day she realized that she *had* made it through the winter of her darkness. Although she had further to go, the overwhelming dark night of the soul was behind her. Even though she didn't feel ready, she did what she had to do, went through the motions, and changed her emotions. She was able to fake it until she was able to truly make it. She pushed through her darkness and woke up to a new dawn.

As important as it is to enter the darkness, there comes a time when the dark becomes destructive rather than constructive. The dark is a temporary dwelling, not a permanent residence. The Jewish tradition says that after losing a parent, sibling, spouse, or child, we're officially designated as mourners for a year with limits on how far we should return to our ordinary lives. For example, parties and festive social affairs are generally avoided. There's a clear difference between venturing into the world for recreation and for responsibility. Nonetheless, there comes a point when it's imperative to rise from the dark and return to the light.

Shards of Light

In Kabbalah, the Jewish mystical tradition, the central thesis is that God is infinite light, but infinite light presents a conundrum. If everything is light, there's no room for anything *but* light. There's no room for you and me and our finite lives. As an act of love, God withdraws some of the light—what Jewish mystics call *tzimtzum*—steps into the background, and creates a place for us to live. This is much like parenting. Raising a child is a process of continual withdrawal. When the child is a newborn, the parent is with her, tending to her every need. As the child becomes a toddler, the parent is still there, following her around and removing obstacles in her path. As the toddler grows, the parent lets her go outside by herself to play, knowing that the child on the monkey bars will eventually fall down and skin her knees. When that child grows older yet, the parent lets her go and sends her off into the world. As that child makes her way through life, her parent may be out of sight, but the child is never out of the parent's mind. The child is always within her loving parent's heart.

God, out of her love for her children, withdrew from this world, making room for her children to move about and exercise free will. Within that freedom is the void that contains the darkness of loneliness and suffering. However, God is still present in the darkness. The sparks of light are obscured, burrowed in human experiences, and they are what the mystics call *nitzozot*, which means "sparks or shards of light." These sparks are there, waiting to be discovered. This is our primary mission in life. God, out of an act of love, gave us the opportunity to become godlike. We have been charged with the sacred task, like God, of shattering darkness by creating light. Within grief and suffering, broken lives and broken hearts, we discover the light released in the sparks. We're here to become spark seekers. We're here to go into the broken world and search our shattered lives for those sparks. We're here to illuminate the darkness for those around us and those who follow in our footsteps.

One Spark at a Time (Shabbat Bags)

Jodi returned to her home in St. Louis to help take care of her dying father. Along with the short days and darkness of winter, the cold reality of her father's illness was sharp and painful for the entire family as his condition deteriorated. When his pain could no longer be managed at home, he entered a hospice house. Jodi told me how, in the first few days at hospice, she sometimes heard a bell tolling, and she wondered what it signaled. It wasn't long before she understood that the bell was rung when a patient died and was being taken out of the building. She watched her father's labored breathing with vigilance and found herself holding her breath when the bell inevitably tolled again.

On a Friday, a few days after his admittance, a volunteer named Linda stopped by the room to say hello. She asked Jodi how she was holding up and said hello to her father. They talked a few minutes, and Linda offered Jodi a *Shabbat* bag from a local synagogue—*Shabbat* is the Hebrew word for the Jewish Sabbath, which begins at sundown on Friday night and ends at sundown on Saturday evening. In it was *challah*, the traditional bread eaten on the Jewish Sabbath, grape juice to make the traditional blessing over the wine, and cookies that symbolized the sweetness and joy of the Sabbath. Linda also brought in electric Shabbat candlesticks for the room. That was the last Sabbath Jodi's dad saw, as he died five days later.

When Jodi returned to Boston after the funeral, she shared this story with me and expressed how moved she had been by this kind gesture. "It was like I hadn't realized how cold I was until this woman I had never met offered up such a loving gift of Sabbath peace. It was as if I was wrapped in warmth." The pain of losing her father was fresh and raw, and she continued to wrestle with the darkness that surrounded her loss. I was reminded of Dejan

Stojanovic, a Serbian poet who wrote, "Fly without wings; dream with open eyes; see in darkness."

After a few months, Jodi came to me with an idea. She knew that it was time to stand from her darkness and find the sparks that would help her move forward. She had a deep desire to pay it forward for the love symbolized in the Shabbat bag she had received at hospice. She instituted a Shabbat bag program in our community and partnered with our synagogue and our local hospice. She delivers these bags herself, and she has created a network of volunteers. While she still feels the pain of her loss, she's creating light for herself, for hospice patients and their families, and for her father. She has a new mission to share with others what she discovered in the darkness, echoing the teachings of the Jewish mystical tradition. The Chassidic parable below illustrates the importance of facing and searching the darkness to find opportunities of light:

> One night, a mystic comes upon a man intensely searching the ground under a street lamp.
>
> "Did you lose something?" inquires the mystic.
>
> "Yes, my keys," responds the man frantically.
>
> So the mystic bends down to help the man search. After much time, he finally asks, "Where exactly did you lose them?"
>
> The man responds, "Over there, in that dark field."
>
> Confused, the mystic says, "Then why are you looking for them over here beneath the light?"
>
> The man explains, "I can't look there—it's too dark!"[38]

By searching in the dark, we will find the keys that can unlock sparks of life and release them into the light of day.

Choosing Light

To be diagnosed with a terminal illness isn't a choice. To lose someone we love isn't a choice, and the darkness that descends upon us when this happens isn't a choice. Our choice resides is whether or not we're willing to face that darkness and enter it. After having entered it, experienced it, and learned from it, will we choose to move back into the light, revealing our own sparks? Avoiding the dark is seductive. Lingering in the dark, or taking up a permanent residence in it, can also be seductive. It has the potential to become our identities.

When the time is right, we must choose to stand up, have the resolve to journey across the bridge from darkness into the light, and let our spirits shine. Marianne Williamson, in *A Return to Love: Reflections on the Principles of a "Course in Miracles,"* says the following:

> Our deepest fear is not that we are inadequate. Our deepest fear is that we are powerful beyond measure. It is our light, not our darkness, that most frightens us...We are all meant to shine, as children do. We were born to make manifest the glory of God that is in us. It's not just in some of us; it's in everyone. And as we let our own light shine, we unconsciously give other people permission to do the same. As we are liberated from our own fear, our presence automatically liberates others.[39]

By facing the darkness, we're able to move toward light, but the initial steps can be terrifying. Everything in us insists that we should turn away from the pain.

It reminds me of what happens when my children scrape their knees. They will push away my hand no matter how gently I use the soap, water, and towel to clean the wound. When I put on the burning antiseptic, the pleas to stop intensify. In their minds, I'm making a painful situation worse, but I'm doing what needs to be done to prevent infection. I know that in order to heal in the long run means that they have to feel more pain in the short run.

This is often the dilemma a mourner must face. Do you turn away from the darkness to avoid feeling even more pain as grief courses through you? If you turn away from the darkness in the hope of avoiding more pain, will you risk an emotional infection? Will the darkness you seek to avoid in the short term have damaging effects in the long term?

Seeking the sparks isn't easy. Those shards of light have the potential to pierce your soul, but we aren't here for a life of ease; we're here for a life of meaning, love, purpose, and authenticity. Being a spark seeker means being real, and being real means being vulnerable. Loving and cherishing others means opening ourselves to loss and grief. This is the cost of being alive. If we're to love and live in the light of day, we must accept the fact we will know loss and darkness. Despite the fantasy that we can love and not lose, we must, sooner or later, face reality.

Like Kisa in the opening story, when the darkness descends, we feel singled out and powerless. We fear that we will be unable to live in a world where our loved ones are no longer present. Jung said, "I am not what has happened to me. I am what I choose to become." Although we have no choice about the pain of death and its darkness, we aren't without choice. No matter how dark our grief and no matter how much we're hurting, we have a choice.

Viktor Frankl, a Holocaust survivor, says the following in *Man's Search for Meaning*:

> We who lived in concentration camps can remember the men who walked through the huts comforting others, giving away their last piece of bread. They may have been few in number, but they offer sufficient proof that everything can be taken from a man but one thing: the last of the human freedoms—to choose one's attitude in any given set of circumstances, to choose one's own way.[40]

Life is about choosing and evolving. Death holds the potential to help us love more fully and live more freely. Jenny, a congregant whose sister, father, and mother all died within a two-year period, told me that she found each loss made her a kinder person. Loss can make us softer even as it makes us stronger and more powerful. Author and speaker Brené Brown says the following:

> Owning our stories can be hard but not nearly as difficult as spending our lives running from them. Embracing our vulnerabilities is risky but not nearly as dangerous as giving up on love and belonging and joy—the experiences that make us the most vulnerable. Only when we're brave enough to explore the darkness will we discover the infinite power of our light.[41]

This is what the Buddha taught Kisa. She could remain a victim, lost forever in her pain, or she could choose to lay her son's body to rest. She could choose to begin laying her grief to rest. She could choose to transform her wandering into a journey back into life with new understanding and purpose. She could choose to reclaim the power of her spirit, her connection to others, and her life's light. And she chooses to become a spark seeker, searching for light amid the darkness. Rumi said, "The wound is the place where the light enters you." The deaths of loved ones can make us stronger or weaker, more loving or less loving. They can enliven us or leave us with one foot in this world and one stuck in the grave. When death's darkness descends upon us, we can choose whether we will transform our wanderings into journeys of healing. We can search for sparks from which we can kindle flames and rediscover life's light.

This doesn't mean that the darkness disappears forever. It's always there—on the other side of the earth, at the end of our days, and bound up with the next loss. In the words of the Greek philosopher Pythagoras, "If there be light, then there is darkness; if cold, heat; if height, depth; if solid, fluid; if hard, soft; if rough, smooth; if calm, tempest; if prosperity, adversity; if life, death." The yin of darkness and the yang of light are complementary energies that move throughout the universe and throughout our lives. By experiencing both light and life *and* darkness and death, we can more fully understand ourselves and live more fully. No one wants the darkness, but it isn't a matter of wanting. Are we going to enter the darkness and search for sparks of light, or will we spend our lives trying to avoid the dark?

Abe was in his eighties when his beloved wife, Bernice, died. What made the situation more painful was the fact his grandson, Steven, was due to have a bar mitzvah later that year. This weighed heavily on everyone, especially Steven. He was very close with his grandparents, and in some ways, they were raising him. He was an only child, and his parents were successful professionals. They weren't around a lot, so Steven spent much of his time with his grandparents. Abe and Bernice were Steven's connection to Judaism. They drove him to Hebrew school and Shabbat services.

It was clear that the loss of Bernice and the coming bar mitzvah were intertwined for the family members. Although they were moving toward that date, they contemplated postponing it or scrapping it altogether. Abe would have none of it. He insisted that they forge ahead.

Fast-forward a few months to the big day of the bar mitzvah. Abe wanted to say a few words. He placed both hands tenderly on Steven's cheeks, looked into his eyes, and gave him a charge like none I had ever seen.

He said, "Steven, as you know, all those years you prepared for this moment, all those times we spoke about this, it's finally here, but not like we expected. We always imagined this moment with Nana standing by my side as we presented the *tallit* (prayer shawl) to you together.

"I know that after Nana died, you wanted to call off the bar mitzvah. I know the rest of the family thought we should postpone this day. I understood why everyone wanted to do this, and for a time, I wanted to postpone it as well. I wouldn't let you do that, my sweet grandson, because I love you too much. I know you have a broken heart. You know I have a broken heart. Our family is broken without Nana, but that is exactly why we had to persevere. There will be more losses. Someday, my boy, I will die, and when that day comes, I want you to promise me that you will not give death the final say. When we face death, as Jews, we say Kaddish. If you look at those words, there's not a mention of death in them. When death comes, what do we shout at the darkness? Not words of more darkness but words of life, love, and light. We say, *"L'chayim,"* (to life) when we raise our glasses high; we shout 'to life' into the face of death.

"You honor Nana by having this bar mitzvah and by celebrating, rejoicing, and living your life. You want to pay tribute to your Nana? Keep doing what you're doing. Keep living. Keep loving. Tonight, during the party at the candle lighting ceremony, light a candle for Nana and then cut a rug in her honor. That's what she'd want you to do. I'm proud of you. She will always be our source of light, and she's shouting from the heavens at this moment, "L'chayim," to you, her sweet Steven."

With those words, a somber occasion was transformed into a celebration of life. Abe's words illuminated that day, and I'm certain they carried Steven and all those in attendance for many days afterward.

We're here to become like Abe, to face our darknesses and transform them. We should do it for ourselves, for the deceased, and most of all, for the living.

Warriors of Light

My mom and dad were married for thirty years before they divorced, roughly ten years before he took his life. In many ways, they were a happily married couple. To this day, my mom shares how she always loved my dad and always will. Unlike some marriages, theirs didn't end due to a lack of love. Although it was my father who ultimately left, my mother taking a stand and giving him an ultimatum was the factor that ended their marriage.

My mom wasn't always so decisive. She was born in an era with a different set of assumptions about what a woman could do and how she should act. Although my home wasn't *Father Knows Best*, it had a traditional framework. My dad had the career and the final say in big decisions, and his temperament set the tone for the house. When Shelly was happy, we were happy. When Shelly was silent and dark, although the kids didn't always know it or feel it, my mom absorbed much of that darkness so that we wouldn't have to. My dad led, and my mom followed.

In the later years of their marriage, as my father began his descent into the darkness, my mom began a journey of her own. She seemed to understand that my father's foundation was crumbling. She began exercising her will and making bigger and bolder decisions for herself and her family. She was finding her own voice and voting with her feet. She went back to school and to work, and she began sharing in the finances. Her name went onto the mortgage, and she became the primary breadwinner after my father's business collapsed. She was beginning to make a stand in her life. She was growing stronger and wiser, and in many ways, she was beginning to live like a spark seeker.

After my parents' marriage collapsed, my dad continued to crumble, but my mom arose out of the ashes like a phoenix. She met a wonderful man who allowed her to be a copilot in their life together, far from the backseat passenger she had been to my dad. My stepfather, Howard, and my mom have gone on to show her children and grandchildren what a healthy, loving relationship looks like.

My mother ascended to great heights professionally, attaining a rarefied position of power in her industry. This was a woman whose husband once balanced her checkbook, but then she began raising tens of millions of dollars for the Jewish community and the state of Israel. At one time, she was too afraid to drive by herself to visit me, a few hundred miles away, when I was in college. After her transformation, she led a dozen trips a year to Israel, Eastern Europe, and the former Soviet Union, sometimes going alone. In the aftermath of my father's dark descent, she became a warrior of light. In the words of Viktor Frankl, "What is to give light must endure burning." My mother endured more than her share of burning. My sister, brother, and I may have lost our patriarch, but we discovered a true matriarch—a woman who exemplified how her spirit could endure and burn brightly as she forged her way through the dark.

As my mother and so many other matriarchs and patriarchs have borne out, there are always sparks of light in the darkness waiting to be discovered. The Jungian psychoanalyst Robert Moore says the following about Japanese samurai warriors:

> The samurai advice was always to "leap" into battle with the full potential of ki or "vital energy" at our disposal. The Japanese warrior tradition claimed that there is only one position in which to face the battle of life: frontally. And it also proclaimed that there was only one direction: forward.[42]

If we're to move forward after loss, there's only one direction. Out there ahead of us are shards of light and sparks of life waiting to be discovered. When we take hold of them, we have the power to illuminate a darkened world for ourselves and others. The sparks within the dark are sparks of hope. The sparks light our way as we search for meaning in our mournings and for ways to lighten our lives and the lives of others.

Sometimes this mission may feel like too much to take on. A Jewish wisdom text explains, "You are not responsible for doing it all; however, you are not free to desist from trying."[43] Your mission is to find your sparks in the darkness and to bring forth their light. The journey from darkness to light begins with one intention, one decision, one action, one spark—and then one after that and one after that. When we gather those sparks, eventually flames ignite. Those flames can be fanned into fire, and those fires can illuminate the way.

Rabbi Schneur Zalman of Liady echoes this when he says, "A little light dispels a lot of darkness." To become a spark seeker is to learn the lessons of the dark and to bring wisdom into the world.

When death's darkness descends after the loss of a loved one, a mission, a purpose, or a calling also descends upon us. The mission is to choose to enter that darkness fully. Our purpose is to seek the sparks of light in the dark depths of grief. The calling is to dispel the darkness and illuminate the way for those beside us. Those who come after us will carry the light forward.

9

ILLUMINATING THE PATH

There's one thing we do know: that man is here for the sake of other men—above all, for those upon whose smiles and well-being our own happiness depends.

—Albert Einstein

My attention is captivated not by how religious traditions differ but by how similar they are, particularly in moments of universal truth. One such moment happens every year at the winter solstice. This is the moment when the darkness that falls across the Northern Hemisphere is at its deepest. Before December 21, the days grow shorter, and the nights grow longer and colder. The dark days of winter have their place, but there comes a point when we can no longer sit in the dark. Various faith traditions rise up, each in its own way, as a response to those darkest days of the year.

There Shall Be Light

Christmas and Hanukkah are millennia-old attempts to dispel the darkness. In celebration of Christmas, trees and homes are decorated with lights, and some people place candles in windows. In celebration of Hanukkah, Jews light the *menorah*, a seven-branched candelabrum. To fulfill the purpose of the holiday, the menorah isn't placed in the interior of the home. Rather, it's set up in the most publicly visible location: a window or the exterior of the house. There it can fully illuminate the darkness and allow others to see. Together, these traditions and their rituals hold thousands of years of shared purpose and power. Each has a metaphor for shining spiritual light and illuminating a darkened world.

Kwanzaa, an African American and Pan-African holiday, began in 1966 in celebration of family, community, and culture. It lasts for seven days, from December 26 through January 1. Like Hanukkah, a central activity is lighting candles on what is called a *mishumaa*.

Hindus across the world celebrate Diwali, which falls on the fifteenth day of the auspicious Hindu month of Kartik—around November on the Gregorian calendar. Diwali falls on a day with no moon. Candles are lit in homes to symbolize the triumph of good over evil. Sikhs, Buddhists, and Jains also celebrate Diwali and offer light amid the darkness.

For the Chinese, the winter solstice is a celebration of the triumph of yang (light) over yin (dark). The holiday, called Dong Zhi, is celebrated during the eleventh lunar month with a ceremony near the family altar, which includes incense, candles, and offerings of prayers.

While these traditions are different, their sentiments are universal. We intuit that the human predicaments of mortality, struggle, and death are to be confronted head on rather than avoided. We stand in opposition to the darkest days of the respective calendars, almost like warriors in battle. The darkness can feel all encompassing, but across continents, religions, cultures, and time, we sense that the best response to the darkness is to dispel it with light.

In many ways, we embody one of the primary messages in the Bible. After the dark of chaos comes the defining moment of the creation story: "And God cried out, there shall be light, and there was light."[44] God's first act was to shatter the darkness through the creation of light. In essence, as the winter solstice or other dark moments on the calendar settle in, we defiantly illuminate the dark and create our own light. The darkness is still out there, and our candles are but specks. Our traditions show that it's our mission to bring light into the darkness. We carry the light into the dark to remind ourselves that a shift is taking place, darkness will diminish, and eventually there will be light again.

Every one of us has this power. We are, as the mystics teach, *b'tzelem Elohim*, which means "in the image of God." We must cry out with every ounce of our beings, "There shall be light!"

Into Me See

In the movie *Avatar*, humans discover strange aliens on a distant planet, but in the end, the humans are strange, and the aliens aren't so alien after all. They teach the humans about their humanity. Their message is best summed up in the way they greet one another. Instead of "Hi," "How are you?" or "What's going on?" they say, "I see you." Their message conveys the following:

- I'm not just looking *at* you or noticing you, but I *see you.*
- I see who you are and what you're facing and enduring.
- I'm here with you, not on the outside looking in but on the inside; you aren't alone.
- I see you because I'm you, you're me, and we're one.

Dr. Wayne Dyer, the author and motivational speaker, teaches that the word *intimacy* conveys this idea. Intimacy, the deep, heartfelt connection between souls, can be written as "into me see."

My father's death deepened my ability to see and recognize pain and enabled me to help those who are suffering. I've come to understand more fully the difference between sympathy and empathy. Whereas sympathy reveals care and concern for another, empathy goes beyond concern and becomes a direct encounter with what the other is experiencing. It's the difference between being on the outside, as an observer looking in, and being on the inside, experiencing what the other person is going through. In those moments, the people we have empathy for are no longer "other"—they are part of us, and we're part of them.

It wasn't until my heart was broken that I discovered empathy. In the words of Jung, "Knowing your own darkness is the best method for dealing with the darknesses of other people." Because of my darkness, I was able to listen to the words of someone else's broken heart and feel his or her brokenness as if it were my own. Pain recognizes pain, and we know intuitively when we're with those who can hold our broken hearts. Pain has the potential to teach us how to move toward empathy and healing when we use it in a skillful way.

Andrea, a member of my synagogue, discovered the importance of empathy in friendship, especially during a time of loss. She made an appointment to talk with me about the anger and frustration she had been feeling toward her friend, Maureen. She stood by Maureen's side during times of loss and tended to Maureen's family in various ways.

When Andrea spent a year flying back and forth to tend to her dying father, she rarely heard from Maureen. Upon her father's death, Andrea received a bouquet of flowers from Maureen and their mutual friend, Carrie, but no reaching out or compassionate concern. Carrie's father had also just died, and Andrea had gone to the funeral the previous day. She found herself standing side by side with Maureen at the cemetery.

After the burial, the rabbi had asked the mourners to make two lines and instructed the family to walk through those lines on their way to their cars. Andrea explained that these two lines symbolized the love and support offered to the family, not only at the funeral but in an ongoing way. The rabbi asked people to be mindful of the family's grief as they experienced their first Thanksgiving without their father, ushered in the new year without him, and faced birthdays and anniversaries without him. Andrea told me that she saw Maureen nodding her head in agreement with the rabbi's words, and that it was painful to watch.

Andrea said, "There I was, standing side by side with Maureen, my father was dead only six months, and she seemed oblivious that the words the rabbi spoke were true of me as well." She believed that if there were ever a time to confront Maureen about how let down she felt, this was the time. She left my office with the intention of sharing her feelings of disappointment with Maureen.

When I saw Andrea again, I asked her how the talk went. She told me that she had decided not to bother calling Maureen. "I was about to make the call, and then I stopped myself. I started thinking that maybe sending flowers and a sympathy card was all that Maureen was able to do at that point in her life." She decided to follow Gandhi's dictate to "be the change that you want to see in the world." Instead of calling Maureen to confront her about how let down she felt during her grieving, she called Carrie so that she could be there in the way she had yearned for Maureen to be there for her.

Andrea said, "I'm making it my priority to be present for my friends in a way that supports their processes and cultivates empathy. I have learned from friends who have taught me what it means to be with someone as witness to their pain. I understand that true empathy doesn't mean trying to fix things, aiming to take away the pain and make it all better, or to send the requisite card; it means to honor whatever your friend is feeling."

Henri Nouwen, a Dutch Catholic priest, says the following:

> When we honestly ask ourselves which persons in our lives mean the most to us, we often find that it is those who, instead of giving advice, solutions, or cures, have chosen rather to share our pain and touch our wounds with a warm and tender hand. The friend who can be silent with us in a moment of despair or confusion, who can stay with us in an hour of grief and bereavement, who can tolerate not knowing, not curing, not healing and face with us the reality of our powerlessness, that is a friend who cares.[45]

Sometimes the people you thought would always be there for you in the greatest time of need aren't there in the way you imagined. Other friends come through for you in a way you never would have guessed. One of the most helpful ways to think about friendships during difficult times is to identify the strengths each person possesses. Many people find it helpful to make a list of the friends who are wonderful to turn to when they need someone to listen to them and share their feelings. Another list may include people who aren't great at listening to emotion but are wonderful at helping in other ways. These are the friends who are happy to drive you to appointments, run errands for you, or help you organize what needs to be done. Another group of friends can be those who are ready to engage in activities with you; they are up for going out to dinner, watching a movie, or spending a day in the city. There are those who are unable to be with you or nurture the friendship in meaningful ways. Letting go of some of these relationships is often healthier in the long run.

We have different friendships that touch different parts of our lives. Knowing which friends to reach out to at different times based on our needs, especially during times of crisis, can create friendships that are more loving and mutually nourishing.

You Never Know

Sometimes our family comes to the rescue. Sometimes it's friends who save us from the pit of despair. Sometimes it's a stranger who appears at the right time, like a guardian angel. You never know.

After my father died, we held a memorial service in the town in which he was living. As I wasn't from there and it was held in the house of someone I didn't know, I didn't think much of it when an unfamiliar young woman walked in. She sat there for a while listening to the impromptu eulogies, the poetry, and the somber songs. As we were wrapping up this fitting tribute, she asked if she could speak.

"You don't know me, and I don't know you," she began. "I hardly knew Shelly, and yet he saved my life."

We were intrigued.

"Shelly used to frequent the café where I work as a barista" she continued. "It's in a part of town caught up in the hustle and bustle of corporate life. The customers are frequently in a hurry and rarely stop to talk. Shelly was there one day when I was particularly down and out. I have suffered from depression most of my adult life, and that particular stretch was tough for me. My little brother had just died. I was a wreck. I was contemplating suicide. I felt so alone.

"Shelly walked into my life. He was always so full of joy and so kind to me and the others in the café. He always asked how I was doing, and he meant it. On that day, seeing how sad I was, he pursued the question and wouldn't take 'fine' for an answer."

How ironic, I thought. "Fine" had been my dad's mantra for so long.

"The café was empty," she said, "so we sat and talked. It was perhaps the most wonderful conversation I have had in my life. My own father would hardly listen to me and certainly hadn't helped me through that difficult time, and yet, here was a man who was practically a stranger to me, owed me nothing, and still sat, listened, empathized, and loved me for who I was and what I was going through. He told me about his mom, his suffering, and his bouts of depression. He opened his heart to me and let me in. As he did, he entered my heart as well.

"I never told Shelly this, but that was a turning point for me. It was the moment I stopped contemplating suicide. He made me want to live. I believe he was an angel of God put in this world at that moment to save my life.

"When I heard that he took his own life, I was heartbroken. It seemed as if one of God's angels had fallen from the sky. I never told him how much it meant to me that our paths had crossed. I never told him how much he meant to me period. I only wish I could have seen that our paths crossed so that I could have helped him the way that he helped me. Maybe I was supposed to see him like he saw me—to save his life as he saved mine."

Throughout the Jewish mystical tradition, there are stories of strangers and beggars wandering into villages and into the lives of individuals. Although these beggars are dressed in disguise, they are always more than what they appear. They aren't beggars, strangers, or mortals; they are the embodiment of divinity in our lives, a reminder that the divine is made manifest at the crossroads and the intersections of our journeys. When we recognize the darkness of loved ones, friends, acquaintances, or strangers, or they recognize ours, we enter that darkness to be with them. We offer them help, sympathetic ears, kind gestures, or smiles. Sparks are released. A little of their darknesses—and often our own—is dispelled, and the divine presence returns to this world. When you seek sparks along your journey, you never know how those sparks might be part of someone else's journey as well.

The rabbis teach, "Whoever destroys a soul, it is considered as if he destroyed an entire world. And whoever saves a life, it is considered as if he saved an entire world."[46] Who is to say that the people we meet on our desert treks, at our café lunches, or across the aisles from us on planes aren't at those intersections of our lives to bring messages and meanings for us or for them? Metaphysics aside, we know that such encounters have impact. Smiles are contagious. Compassion is infectious, and human beings respond to the energy around them. You never know who is here to help you along your path. You never know whose journey you might be part of.

Jessica, a woman at our synagogue, told me about the time she was on a flight to Florida. The plane had not yet taken off. An older woman sat across the aisle from her, and she overheard the woman talking on her cell phone—her father had just died. Jessica saw the pain on the woman's face and heard the voice mail she left for her husband, telling him the news. The woman then called her brother and tearfully told him the news.

Jessica didn't want to be intrusive and tell the woman that she overheard what she was going through, yet at the same time, she felt that if she had just heard that news about her own father, she wouldn't want to sit alone with it for a three-hour flight, unable to talk to anyone about what she had just learned. She decided to reach out and speak to the woman across the aisle.

Jessica caught the woman's eyes and told her that she couldn't help overhearing her on the phone. She said that she was so sorry for the loss of her father. She told the woman that she couldn't know what would serve her right then, but if at any time during the flight she felt like talking, she was there for her.

The woman held Jessica's hand and thanked her. She then shared that she was on the plane to visit her father who was in a nursing home in Florida. She couldn't believe that she was so close to seeing him but would never sit with him again.

The two women ended up talking for the entire flight. During that time, despite living over forty miles from one another, they discovered they had a mutual friend. About a month later, Jessica received a card from the woman—she had asked the mutual friend for Jessica's address. On her card, she wrote that she couldn't imagine how she would have gotten through that flight without Jessica reaching out and offering the space to process all that her heart was holding. She told Jessica that she would always think of her as an "angel in flight" who appeared exactly when she was needed.

The examples of how families, friends, community members, colleagues, neighbors, acquaintances, or even strangers lift one another up, become sparks in one another's darknesses, and illuminate the paths for one another amid grief are endless and breathtaking. What if we aren't random, disconnected beings making our way through life without signposts or road maps? What if there are angels around us, manifesting in myriad forms? Maybe the question isn't whether they are here but if we ready to see them.

There are sparks in the dark, and often those sparks are found in a tender touch, a compassionate glance, or a gentle smile. The next time people cross our paths, pour our coffees, or ask us for directions, maybe we'll respond differently, particularly when we're in a dark place. Maybe we'll rethink the possibilities of our interactions with strangers, friends, and families. Maybe we're not always the ones receiving the message. Sometimes we're the messengers of hope: living, breathing angels on earth who can shift a moment or change a life.

In the words of Anne Frank, "Look at how a single candle can both defy and define the darkness." Maybe we're each that single candle, that flickering spark illuminating for someone what otherwise would be cold, lonely darkness. "I see you" isn't just a beautiful way to say hello and good-bye; it's the mission statement of a spark seeker.

Lean on Me

The word *religion* comes from the Latin root *ligare*, which means "to connect or to bind," as in the word *ligament*. It doesn't specify what is being connected; there are many connections to be made. There's the connection to God, the divine, or the one. There's the connection to the pastor, priest, guru, imam, or rabbi. There's the connection to the church, ashram, mosque, or Zen center. There's the connection to the community itself. As it says in the Hebrew Bible, "Make for me a *mikdash* (a sacred space), and I will dwell *b'tocham* (within you)."[47] The Jewish mystics point out that if what is sacred is the place, it should have read, "I will dwell within it" rather than "I will dwell within you." The space isn't sacred; bricks aren't holy, and mortar isn't divine. What is sacred and divine are the people within those walls, the interactions that take place between flesh and blood within that space, and the relationships formed within that community. Often it's less about connecting to "the one" and more about connecting to *someone*. Religion is about making connections, and any group or organization that fosters relationships, regardless of dogma or proclamations of belief, becomes a mikdash. Any institution committed to compassion and love brings us into the heart of relationships.

This was brought home to me on the holiest day on the Jewish calendar, Yom Kippur. It's the Jewish Day of Atonement, and Kol Nidre is the evening service that ushers it in. It opens with the Aramaic words that translate as "all vows." Kol Nidre reminds us to be mindful of the vows we make and to strive to fulfill those vows.

Recently during Kol Nidre, I spoke to my congregation about my family's story. I shared my journey of darkness, told them about my grandmother's and father's suicides, and spoke of how these events shaped my life personally and professionally. I told them of the studies that show the rising incidence of suicide and the new research showing a strong link between suicide and weakened social ties. I made the case, from examples throughout the Torah to examples in our present day, that despite how much Americans value self-reliance and independence, there's a shadow side to this mind-set. Going it alone, day in and day out, isn't sustainable. Eventually our burdens become too great, and we burn out. We may experience depression or anxiety and become isolated, and in a vicious cycle, we retreat even more, perpetuating the darkness. This is what happened to my father. And in the days before my Kol Nidre sermon, this happened when a woman in our community took her life.

I shifted the talk to vows. Along with over a thousand congregants, my wife and my oldest child, Yehudah, then eleven, sat in the sanctuary. I stood at the pulpit and said, "I vow I will never make the choice that my grandmother and father made, and I vow to do everything in my power to make sure that no one in my family believes this is a viable choice." Looking toward my wife and son, I said, "I will never leave you by taking my life."

I said that this wasn't only about my personal vows but about our vows as a community. "No matter who you are, no matter how lonely you might feel, and no matter how bad it might seem, *U'vacharta B'Chayim* (I vow to choose life)."

I asked the congregation to say it with me. Our voices rose up as we said, "I vow to choose life."

I talked about feelings of despair and people in our midst who were living in darkness. I talked about how it was our duty to reach out to them. "Tonight we must all vow to speak up. Say it with me."

The congregation said in unison, "I vow to speak up."

I went on, "Tonight we must all vow to speak out. Say it with me."

The congregation chanted, "I vow to speak out."

I said, "Tonight we must all vow to shatter the silence and speak about what we believe is unspeakable: depression, darkness, death, and suicide. Together we say, 'I vow to shatter the silence.'" We repeated these words and took the vows.

I explained that it was our duty to do the following:

- Remember and reach out to the stranger in need.
- Remember and reach out to the orphan (any age) who is alone.

- Remember and reach out to the widow or widower who is lost.
- Remember and reach out to friends who are battling depression.
- Remember and reach out to colleagues struggling with physical illnesses.
- Remember and reach out to our neighbors who are alone.

I said, "It is time for us to make new vows as a country, a community, a congregation, as families, and as individuals. Tonight on Kol Nidre, we must vow to open our hearts. Say it with me: 'I vow to open my heart.' Tonight on Kol Nidre, we must vow to open our hands. Say it with me: 'I vow to open my hand.' Tonight on Kol Nidre, we must vow to reach out to those in need. Say it with me: 'I vow to reach out to those in need.'"

I concluded by saying that we speak these vows that might have saved my grandmother, father, and countless others because a vow might save one person, which is like saving the entire world.

I looked at the sea of faces before me and announced the vow. We all sang Bill Withers's song, "Lean on Me." As we sang, I said, "If you are willing, please stand if you've been touched by suicide. If you've been touched by the death of a loved one, please rise. If you or someone you know is facing physical challenges, please rise. If you or someone you know is facing emotional darkness and pain, please stand."

There wasn't one person left seated in the room. Spontaneously, people began placing their arms around the people next to them. As I looked across the room, there was a sacred community of souls linking themselves together in vows, in words, in song, and in love.

When the darkness descends, we all need someone to lean on. At the same time, we all have opportunities in our lives to be the ones others will lean on. There's the old saying that "it is better to give than to receive." I think it's equally good to give and to receive.

Kabbalah comes from the Hebrew word *l'kabel,* which means "to receive." The Hebrew word for blessing, *barchu,* shares its root with the word *beirach,* which means "knee." As we receive blessings, we humble ourselves, bend our knees in supplication, and show our readiness to receive. Both giving and receiving are active. In giving, we also receive, and in receiving, we also give. Sometimes we're the ones doing the leaning, and sometimes we're the ones others lean against. It's a fluid relationship that moves people forward as light and love are ignited. Within both, we can find sparks in the darkness.

Becoming Bodhisattvas

There are the people in our lives who don't hide from the darkness. They sit with us in the dark and gently help us to find our sparks of light. They remind us of the best of what humanity has to offer. In different religious traditions, such men and women go by various names. In Judaism, they are called a *tzaddik;* in Islam, *wali;* in Hinduism, *guru;* in Christianity, *saint;* and in Buddhism, *bodhisattva.* Whatever you call them, each one has been through the darkness and emerged into enlightenment, discovering the light within themselves. Rabbi Menachem Mendel of Kotsk says the following:

> One who seeks to be a *rebbe* (master teacher) must ascend mountains and descend valleys to seek hidden treasures, to knock on the gates, many gates, until the heart breaks, until the body crumbles, until heaven and earth collapse, while he maintains his way.[48]

These are people whose lights are hard won but who, instead of keeping those lights to themselves or remaining blissfully in light, return to the darkness to help others find their sparks. They are the embodiment of what it means to be a spark seeker.

We don't have to become tzaddiks or bodhisattvas to be spark seekers; we just have to understand that we aren't here simply for ourselves. The Hebrew word for "work," *avodah*, is the same word for "prayer." Our true work, regardless of our professions, is to serve ourselves and to serve others through offering our lights. When we serve, however that might be, we enter the realm of the divine. We fulfill our ultimate purpose, the reason why we're here, and the reason why we're alive.

There's a story about a rabbi who asked his students, "When is it at dawn that you can tell the light from the darkness?"

One student replied, "When I can tell a goat from a donkey."

"No," answered the rabbi.

Another said, "When I can tell a palm tree from a fig."

"No," answered the rabbi.

"What is the answer?" his students pressed.

"When you look into the face of every man and every woman and see your brother and your sister. Only then have you seen the light. All else is darkness."

Being spark seekers means that we're ready and willing to open our eyes and hearts to the light, even amid the darkness. It means seeing that our lives are bound up with family, friends, and strangers, as well as those who are no longer on this earth. We have the opportunity, indeed the blessing, to choose to move forward even when we feel bereft in our grief.

In the parable of the mustard seed, Kisa learns what we all know but try mightily to keep at bay: all is impermanent, and every one of us will die. Though this reality often leaves us with fear and dread, it can also lead us to live more fully, freely, and lovingly. How precious this life is and yet how fleeting, whether we live on this earth for ten years or one hundred years. The awareness of our limited time can propel us into finding sparks in the darkness, such as reveling in the budding crocus emerging from the damp earth, crying tears of joy at the birth of a child, and shedding tears of sorrow at the death of a loved one. It's a cycle, and we're part of it. Day turns to dusk, dusk to night, night to dawn, and dawn back to day. Each moment has a place in our lives and a place in our deaths.

We will all know loss and grief, so the question is how we can move forward even in our deepest grieving? We move forward by knowing our darknesses, moving through them, and finding the sparks of light that can guide us forward. As we travel that path, we can be lights for others, just as they can be lights for us. We can serve one another as a reflection of the truths of life and death and the spirit of endurance. Step by step, we can journey through mourning into the possibilities of a new day.

George Bernard Shaw wrote the following:

> Life is no brief candle to me. It is a sort of splendid torch, which I have got hold of for the moment, and I want to make it burn as brightly as possible before handing it on to future generations.[49]

CHAPTER 10:

CARRYING THE FIRE

If you look deeply into the palm of your hand, you will see your parents and all generations of your ancestors. All of them are alive in this moment. Each is present in your body. You are the continuation of these people.

—Thich Nhat Hanh

Within the pantheon of childhood experiences, there's the universal game of hide-and-seek.

Hide-and-Seek

Though most of us have joyous memories of this game, I also have a sad memories associated with it. One event took place when I was about eight years old. It was a summer evening, dusk was settling in, and the neighborhood kids and I had been playing hide-and-seek for hours. During the final round, I found a hiding spot so good that my friends eventually called it quits. The only problem was that they didn't tell me they were going home. I waited until it was beginning to get dark. Eventually I got up and realized that I was all alone. *How could that be?* I thought. *I did what I was supposed to do: I hid.* They failed to uphold their end of the bargain, and I was forgotten and left alone.

No one wants to be forgotten in a childhood game, in this lifetime, or after death. It's why we carve our names on trees, doodle our initials on scraps of paper, or have inscriptions etched on our tombstones. It's why it's so tempting to put a footprint into wet cement. It's why we take pictures, create scrapbooks, and pass down heirlooms. We do these because we want the world to know that we were here. We want our voices to be heard after they have been silenced by death.

To be forgotten means that we're expendable. It means facing the harsh thought that we're replaceable. In some ways, we know we're replaceable. If something happens to us, others will step in and do the tasks and functions we've spent our lives doing. No matter what we do or how good we are at our tasks, when we're gone, the world moves on.

For me, and I suspect many others, this truth is bearable. It would be nice to be irreplaceable, but I know that I'm not. It would be meaningful to be remembered after I'm dead, but I can accept that I will be forgotten by the world. What makes my heart ache is the thought of being forgotten in my immediate world. I'd want my wife, children—and grandchildren, if that day comes—friends, and community to move on, but I want to say, "Move on, but don't forget me. Carry me in a way that serves my memory and your spirit."

This fear of being forgotten reminds me of my friend Irwin, who died a few years ago. He was a wildly successful businessman. Everyone I knew loved him for his exuberant personality and his philanthropic spirit. Within his community he was almost single-handedly responsible for the building of hospitals, schools, and synagogues. He had children and grandchildren who adored him and a community that respected him, and yet he periodically showed up at my office and wanted to talk, agitated about something. Although he never took the subject of death head on, we danced around it. He worried tremendously about his legacy—impacting his community, making a difference in the world, and being remembered by his family. He said, "Baruch, you always wonder if you're doing enough." Despite the institutions built by his generosity and his loving and giving spirit, he continued to worry about being remembered. He tirelessly worked to leave his mark in a self-imposed race against his unspoken fears.

Irwin has passed on, but his legacy endures. Buildings may or may not still bear his name, but his children, grandchildren, and community remember him for what he embodied. If he could have internalized this in life, it might have brought him a greater sense of peace in how he approached death.

Those who are facing death have their own questions and fears, and those who survive the loss of loved ones are struggling with their own questions as well. They try to find their way in a new normal after those they loved have died. They ask themselves the questions, "How will I move forward now? How could I ever replace what he was to me? Should I move forward even if I could? What happens if I can't find my way? What happens if I forget?"

On numerous occasions, I've had the painful privilege of sitting with the bereaved: the widow or widower, the child of a deceased parent, or the parent of a child who has died. There's often a shared sentiment that to move forward implies to move beyond or, worse yet, to leave their loved ones behind. This fear can leave them paralyzed. They are terrified that if they move forward, they will forget or feel tremendous guilt. It implies forgetting or betrayal. For many, moving beyond the darkness means leaving their loved ones behind.

Carrying the Dark

I had known Rick and Mimi for only a few months. They were among the first people that I met at my first synagogue as a young rabbi.

Rick was in the midst of winding down his illustrious career as a doctor. Mimi was a devoted wife, the mother of their three children, and the embodiment of the saying, "Behind every great man, there is a great woman." She was a great woman, and they had created a beautiful life together.

After forty years of marriage, they were making preparations to retire and buy their dream home in the country. Most of all, they were looking forward to "their" time after decades of running a medical practice and raising a family. Their eyes twinkled like newlyweds as they held hands and told me that after all the years together, they were even more in love than the day they married. They were almost giddy about the next chapter of their life together.

Out of nowhere, with no symptoms or family history, Mimi was diagnosed with late-stage cancer. In a matter of weeks, she was dead.

The community was devastated. Mimi had been a beautiful lady, shining such a bright light, and her family was swept into darkness. I didn't realize at the time that we were witnessing two deaths: Mimi's and Rick's. Days turned into weeks, weeks into months, and months into years.

Nearly three years after Mimi's passing, Rick was breathing but hardly alive. Not knowing what to do with himself, he went back to work, but he was so depressed that he was forced to retire again. He gave up on the dream home and all of his other dreams. He disappeared from the synagogue, from the community, and from the lives of his friends. He hardly spoke to his own children. Although he answered the phone when they called, he rarely called them. Despite showing up at family gatherings and joyous occasions, like the births of his grandchildren, he was there in body but not in spirit. His children called me to see if I could help him move on.

Visiting Rick at his home was like something out of a movie. When Mimi died, the shades were pulled shut during the mourning period, and they were never raised again. On many levels, Rick lived in the dark. His home was dimly lit and dreary. Three years after Mimi's passing, nothing of hers had been touched. He pointed out her possessions as if they were part of a display at the Metropolitan Museum of Art.

It was more than a thousand days since Rick's beloved wife left his side, but to him, it was as raw as if she had died the day before. Every suggestion I made about moving back out into the world was met with angry opposition. On some level, he was proud of the way he had served her for those years. He was convinced that to leave the darkness of his grief behind was a statement about his love for her. He had made it his life's purpose to carry the darkness—in his mind, it was what a loving, devoted spouse should do.

Although Rick's example is extreme, he's far from alone. I have met widows and widowers, children, and parents who not only buried a loved one but, like Rick, buried much of themselves. They feel that their loyalties are to the dead, not the living. They are driven to hold on to the darkness, and by doing so, they believe that they are serving a sacred duty. In many ways they are right. A piece of them dies alongside their loved ones.

With this primal call to carry our loved ones, we intuit that there's something profound to be done for them after they are gone. What Rick and others like him miss isn't the call but the deeper meaning and nature of the call. We're called to remember our loved ones and carry them with us in a way that promotes life while honoring death. The call is about carrying the light of our loved ones forward into life rather than carrying the darkness as a tribute to their deaths.

In Genesis, as the patriarch Jacob is dying, he calls his children and grandchildren to his bedside and blesses them. He tells them that his final request is to be buried in the family burial plot that his grandfather Abraham purchased in the land of Canaan. He makes his son Joseph promise that he will honor his wishes. Joseph fulfills his father's request, and when Joseph is about to die, he also gathers his sons and community and makes the same request: "And Joseph took an oath from the people of Israel, saying, 'God will certainly visit you, and you shall carry up my bones from here.'"[50]

Jacob and Joseph weren't just asking to have their bones transported. In Hebrew, the word for "bones," *atzamot*, also means "essence." What they wanted—and what most of us want—was to be remembered. More than our bodies to be interred or scattered in the proper places, we want to have our families and communities remember us by carrying our essences forward.

Never Forget

When the dying make these requests, the point is more about how those left behind will commit to remembering them. Joseph fulfilled his father's request with a sense of urgency. Immediately after the initial mourning period, Joseph begged Pharaoh to allow him to return to Canaan and to carry his father home: "Now therefore let me go up, I beg you, and bury my father, and I will return."[51]

Joseph was driven to honor his father's final request. It motivated him to rise from what must have been a great darkness as he mourned his father. We wonder what he might have done with his grief had his father not charged him with such a great task. Would he have risen from the darkness so quickly and so passionately? Would he have lingered in his grief for too long, potentially losing himself in that darkness? Maybe this was less about Jacob and more about Joseph. Jacob was a patriarch, and patriarchs in the Torah and in life, particularly at deathbed blessings, don't mince words. What they speak is often less about their fears of dying and more about their concerns for those who will live when they are gone. Maybe his mission wasn't so much for the dying as it was for the living.

Joseph receives his father's charge as a teaching, and it helps him to understand his role as a dying patriarch. Upon his death, he imparts the same sacred, purposeful task on his children and community. It becomes a cycle of duty to remember and carry forward the essence of those we've loved and lost. What happens when we can't find a way to integrate the memory and carry the essences of our loved ones? This is what happened in the story of Joseph.

The book of Genesis ends with Joseph's wish unfulfilled. It closes with these words: "And Joseph was put in a coffin in Egypt."[52] In Hebrew, the word for Egypt is *Mitzriam*, meaning "narrow place" or "place of constriction." The story of Joseph's children, the Israelites, is about a people who forgot their sacred duty to those who came before them. With each passing moment of forgetfulness, their world narrowed, their darkness increased, and eventually they lost their way. They were slaves in exile.

In the words of the Jewish mystic Ba'al Shem Tov, "Forgetfulness leads to exile. Memory is the source of redemption." It isn't until Moses, having lived in self-imposed exile, returned to Egypt to save the Israelites that their real exodus, and the journey from forgetting to remembering, began.

In Hebrew, there's no word for history. The closest word, *zachor*, means "memory." What is the difference between history and memory? England's former chief rabbi Dr. Jonathan Sacks says in *The Chief Rabbi's Haggadah*, "History is his story—an event that happened sometime else to someone else. Memory is my story—something that happened to me and is a part of who I am. History is information. Memory, by contrast, is part of identity."[53]

Moses redeemed his people, leading them out of the place of constriction and darkness, by redeeming himself. He rose out of his darkness and remembered who he was: an Israelite. He remembered his father, his father's father, and his duty to carry their essences forward. He returned to Egypt to help free the slaves and prepare the Israelites to make their exodus: "Moses took the bones of Joseph with him because Joseph had made the Israelites swear an oath."[54]

My youngest child, at two and a half, is at the age where he's too heavy to hold but too little to keep up with the rest of us. When he can no longer keep up, he tugs on my heartstrings with his impassioned plea, "Uppies, uppies!" *Uppies* means, "Pick me up and carry me home." As adults, we all need uppies now and again. We need loved ones to pick us up and carry us through life's darkness. We need them to carry us through our grief and back into life. We need them, after we're gone, to carry us home.

The late Rabbi Abraham Joshua Heschel says the following in his book, *Who Is Man?*:

> The authentic individual is neither an end nor a beginning but a link between ages, both memory and expectation. Every moment is a new beginning within a continuum of history. It is facetious to segregate a moment and not to sense its involvement in both past and future. Humbly the past defers to the future, but it refuses to be discarded. Only he who is an heir is qualified to be a pioneer.[55]

The Israelites' exodus wasn't merely a physical journey from Egypt to Israel. It was one from exile to redemption, from forgetting to remembering, and from darkness to light. By acknowledging to whom he was an heir, Moses became a pioneer. By remembering where they had come from, the Israelites resumed their journey to the Promised Land. In the physical and spiritual act of carrying Joseph, their beloved father and ancestor, they were able to move the story forward.

Carrying My Father

When my father died, one of my first responses was to become a collector and nearly a hoarder. It was my mission to gather everything he created or touched. I scoured my home for pictures, and when I found them, I scanned them into the computer for back-up. I searched for letters, and every one I found was like winning the lottery. I devoured them. I treated anything with his handwriting on it like a treasured gift. A sticky note with the words *I love you*, a to-do list—it didn't matter, because it was my dad's. They were his words in his handwriting. His hand had touched the paper, and what were merely words on paper took on sacred meaning. Like Joseph, something within called me to serve my father's memory. I felt charged to carry his memories forward; I wanted to keep him alive.

No matter how many pictures I stockpiled, it was never enough. It dawned on me that the pictures would eventually fade or be lost. Even if they were passed down, at some point they would be forgotten. The artifacts of his life that I crammed into a shoebox, the letters I discovered, anything he touched, and any product of his hand would someday disappear. I vowed to talk to my children about him and to tell them his stories. I even saved a voice mail message he left for me, but no amount of audio or video satisfied what I was searching for.

After a year of furiously writing about him, trying to articulate every memory, life lesson, and bit of anger, joy, or pride, I realized that none of it would keep my dad alive. The sights, the sounds, the memories, and even the will to keep on writing about him began to dissipate. I was forgetting, and that was perhaps the most painful part of losing him.

As I journeyed through the darkness, I began to understand. Forgetting is natural and human. Jacob didn't expect Joseph to remember everything about him. Joseph couldn't have imagined that his progeny would remember the details of his life, his face, or ultimately even his name—do you know the names of your great-great-grandparents? However, they could remember something deeper and carry forward something more profound.

I was charged with carrying forward my father's *atzamot*, the essence in his bones. If his essence was to survive and if I was to truly serve him, I would have to reorient from death's darkness to life's light. I was being called to do what Rick (Mimi's widower) and all survivors are called to do after loved ones die. It's about moving through the darkness and, when the time is right, moving into the light of life.

The Pulitzer Prize–winning author Cormac McCarthy brings this idea home in his book *The Road*, which was made into a screenplay. It's a story about a father and his young son. They survive a nuclear holocaust in which the majority of humanity is wiped out. A handful of stragglers try desperately to stay alive by foraging for food and shelter in the dangerous environment. The father thinks about taking his son's life and then his own to escape their miserable reality. As he's about to die, not of his own hand but from the ravages of his physical condition, and leave his precious child alone in a cruel world, the following conversation ensues:

Boy: I want to be with you.

Man: I want to be with you, too, but I can't.

Boy: Please.

Man: You have to go off on your own now. You have to carry the fire.

Boy: I don't know how to.

Man: Yes, you do. You know everything about it.

Boy: Is it real? The fire? Papa?

Man: Yes, it is.

Boy: Where is it? I don't know where it is.

Man: Yes, you do.

Boy: Where?

Man: It's inside you. It was always there.[56]

This passage came to me nearly a year after wandering through the stages of grieving for my father. It came as I was furiously trying to carry my father as Joseph carried his dad or as Moses carried Joseph. When I read this passage, I understood my mission in a way that I had been unable to articulate. My dad was calling out to me. His bones were calling out to me. His essence was calling out to me, but it wasn't coming from outside me. It was within me. I was ready to go deep into my divine spark, the fire within me, and let it guide me through the darkness. My father's essence was calling out to me just like a loved one's spirit may call out to you.

Jacob said to Joseph, "Promise me that you'll carry my bones." Joseph said to his children, "Promise me that you'll carry my essence." We all say to our loved ones, whether we realize it or not, "Promise me that you'll carry me." In our own ways, we plead for uppies: "When I'm dead, promise me that you'll pick me up and carry me home."

Constructive and Destructive Flames

Millions of people watch the Olympic torch as it passes from runner to runner across cities and countries. It's mesmerizing to watch the flame traveling a large distance to reach a spot dedicated to the celebration of the triumph of the human spirit. In many ways, that image concretizes what it means to carry the fire of our loved ones. The torch we use is the chamber of our hearts. We carry the flame forward when we share our loved ones' essences with the world.

It's also our duty to be wise about the fire we carry. Fire has both constructive and destructive properties, and the fire our loved ones carried is most often a mix of both. It's our charge, for ourselves and the world we live in, to cultivate the positive qualities of our loved ones' fires. It's equally important to let destructive fires burn out.

The book of Genesis isn't only a tale of great men and women who created fire and taught their children to carry it. It's also a case study of dysfunctional families and parents passing down destructive fires. Part of what we take with us from these myths is a call to break the cycle of dysfunction and darkness.

For all of his faults, my father was a source of inspiration as he blazed his path. He was an affectionate father. My siblings and I were showered with hugs, kisses, love, and nurturing words. From what I was told, my grandfather showed no affection and gave few words of appreciation or love to my father, even when he was a boy. It wasn't fully my grandfather's fault—his father, Baruch, my namesake, also refrained from showing affection. Each succeeding generation moved forward in its own way, carrying constructive fires but often carrying destructive ones as well. My father was able to break this cycle and put out the destructive family fires. His affection for his children saturated our lives, and he created positive flames of warmth.

The Torah commands us to honor our parents, not simulate their lives or obey their examples. Sometimes to honor others means to hold on to their constructive flames while putting out the destructive ones. I realized that to carry my father's essence, I had to differentiate between the constructive and destructive fires in my heart.

So much of his life was spent cultivating his flame and illuminating the darkness of those in his midst. For most of his life, he was a good son, man, husband, father, brother, friend, employee, boss, colleague, Jew, citizen, and human being. These were the life-affirming qualities that I wanted to carry forward, but in some of his key moments, the fire of who he was scorched the earth around him. It burned me, and others, and ultimately consumed his life. These were the destructive flames that I had a duty to extinguish.

Although all losses are different, and suicide is an extreme example, most relationships aren't composed solely of constructive fires. As important as it is to carry them forward, it's incumbent upon us to put down the destructive fires as well.

Beth made an appointment to meet with me about a month after her father's death. She was struggling with her loss but felt her pain even more because her father had been such a difficult man. "People make assumptions about my experience. They keep talking about how hard it is to lose a parent who's been such a role model and who guided us from childhood into adulthood, but they don't understand what it was like with my dad."

She said that her father had a quick temper and that she never knew what might set him off. Though she loved him, she didn't like having to walk on eggshells or fearing when his temper might flare. Her father had made it implicitly clear that he would have preferred a son who played sports. He never came to her dance recitals, although she was often featured in solos.

As she spoke about her relationship with him, we explored how her experiences helped to shape who she was as a mother. We talked about how each time she showed up for her son's baseball game or her daughter's swim meet, she was putting out her dad's flames of hurt for not showing up. Each time she demonstrated patience rather than anger, she shifted the parent-child relationship that she had known. She told me that one thing she loved about her father was his wonderful sense of humor. It was something that she had inherited from him and shared with her children.

Beth remembered planting tomatoes with him every year when she was growing up, picking them off the vine together when they were ripe, and enjoying them with their dinner. She loved the idea of carrying this tradition on with her children. She felt this would be a great way to continue growing the loving memories she had of those times with her dad in the garden. By identifying what she needed to put down or pick up, she was able to move forward with a sense of purpose in a way that honored her father. She was ready to carry the fire.

Ted had to learn how to put down his destructive fires in order to resume his life after his wife died. Ted and Mary had been married for fifteen years. It was a second marriage for both of them, and they were deeply in love. Ted was crushed when Mary died suddenly from a brain aneurism, and he suffered even more at the discoveries he made after she died.

A few weeks after the funeral, he stumbled onto an e-mail account and learned that Mary had been leading a double life. Discovery after discovery confirmed that she had been involved with another man. This wasn't the woman he had known, loved, and been mourning.

When he came to see me, he said, "I don't know if I'm supposed to mourn Mary or not. If so, which one do I mourn—the one I believed to be my wife or the one who was cheating on me? Are they different people, or are they the same?"

Although there was no easy answer, Ted and I agreed that he loved his wife, and the wife that he was in love with loved him as well. He would always carry his wife's fire in his heart. He realized that just as there were two women to sort out, there were two types of fire. His beloved wife was a white fire, a source of inspiration, warmth, light, and life. The woman who betrayed him was a black fire that brought destruction. We agreed that his journey through mourning would entail sorting the white fire from the black fire. He could carry one forward, protect it, and draw strength from it, and he could let go of the darker, destructive fire. It would be difficult and painful, but he knew which fire to cultivate if he was to move forward.

When loved ones die, we often have to choose which fires to carry and which to place in the grave. We learn from our loved ones' virtues, accomplishments, and white fires, but we also learn from their vices, failures, and the destruction of the black fires. We can override the destructive fires of our loved ones and use them as reminders of the negative qualities that destroy life rather than affirm it. We should work toward the sacred task of extinguishing the dysfunctional black flames that burn too hot and cause too much pain. At the same time, we have the opportunity, indeed the mission, to carry the constructive white fires. Both aspects allow us to remember our loved ones and move forward in our lives. When we can carry the sparks of our loved ones' goodness into our lives, we cultivate the fires for ourselves, and future generations, with warmth, safety, and light.

The suffering we endure with the loss of loved ones holds in it the opportunity to reflect on our own lives' fires and to fan our constructive flames. If we tend to our fires, knowing when we need more warmth or need to scale back, we can shine our lights even more brightly while we live. In the process, we can grow in understanding, patience, love, openness, and wisdom. When we do this work, we offer the gift of these precious flames for those we love and who will one day carry our fires.

CONCLUSION:

THE LIGHT OF DAY

"My heart is so small
it's almost invisible.
How can you place
such big sorrows in it?"
"Look," he answered,
"your eyes are even smaller,
yet they behold the world."

—Rumi

In the Buddhist parable at the beginning of this book, we met Kisa. She was brokenhearted because her son had died. She knocked on the villagers' doors, looking for mustard seeds from a house where no one had died in order to bring her son back to life.

The Wholeness of a Broken Heart

At one point in our grieving, we are, like Kisa, broken and searching for the impossible: to bring our loved ones back to life. As we journey through our grief, we become those villagers. We're the ones who can offer mustard seeds only from homes that have known grief. We're the grandmother or grandfather, mother or father, husband or wife, sister or brother, or child or friend who will say that we have loved and lost. We will speak of our loved ones and share their stories, and we will be among those who learn to love in separation rather than in presence. To become spark seekers is to recognize that our losses aren't closed doors in our lives but openings in our hearts. When our hearts are shattered by death, we have the opportunity to become whole.

This is far from our natural reactions. In nature, things retract at the threat of danger. They close up, limit their exposures, and hide their most vulnerable sides. Our natural reactions at such times are to run, hide, or defend ourselves against the onslaught of emotions. Our first response is to protect our vulnerable hearts.

Upon the death of an immediate family member, the Jewish tradition of *kriah*—the tearing of one's clothes—physically demonstrates brokenheartedness. When loved ones are ripped away from us, pieces of ourselves are ripped away as well. The Hebrew word for "vulnerability," *pah-gee-ah*, is almost the same word for "wound," *pee-gu-ah*. Our wounds expose our hearts and make us vulnerable. A person's natural reaction to loss is to cover the wounds and conceal his or her heart.

We must rebel against our nature and let our broken hearts be exposed. Physical wounds must be exposed to air to heal, and emotional wounds need similar exposure at some point as well. There's no shame in brokenness. On the contrary, it's what will make us whole. In the words of Rabbi Menachem Mendel of Kotzk, "There is nothing so whole as a broken heart."

After a loss, it's imperative to allow the brokenness and accept it not as an end but a beginning. It's a new reality with new opportunities for growth, goodness, and meaning.

The Edge of Grief

There's a metaphor that speaks to the healing borne from brokenness:

When you break a glass on the floor, you have to be careful when you clean it up. The glass is sharp, so as you pick it up, piece by piece, you have to go slowly and touch the glass cautiously. Even the slightest encounter with it can pierce your skin. The shards are harsh, and the edges cut deeply.

Now imagine that those pieces of glass have been thrown into the ocean. They are at the mercy of the current. At times, the ocean roars with forceful waves, and the glass is tossed and thrown along with the rocks and sand. At other times, the ocean is gentle, and the glass is stroked by the rhythm of the tide. Just as the gentle ocean lulls the glass, another storm hits, and the glass is pushed by the force of the currents. At some point, the ocean quiets, and the flow is again soft. The waves flow, like inhalation and exhalation, as they arrive at the shore and hug the sand.

There you are on a sunny day, walking along the seashore. Just in front of you, amid pebbles and periwinkle shells, is a piece of sea glass. You bend down to pick it up, marveling at your good fortune. You hold it in your hands, feeling its smoothness and the places where it has a slight ridge. You can rub it on all sides because the edges have become smooth, and you can hold it in your hand without fear of injury. Holding it feels fortifying and strengthening.

We seek these brilliant pieces of sea glass because they echo the beauty of survival, resiliency, and hope. With tenderness and love, you hold the sea glass and learn its unique features. Once the edges were jagged and sharp, but now, through the combination of adversity and time, the edges are softly rounded. The glass is beautiful, precious, and whole.

That is how grief can change, and these are the edges of grief. When we hold pieces of sea glass, we hold what was part of something broken and painful to touch. After glass is tossed in the ocean of life, it becomes stronger. Each piece we find tells us that we, too, are treasures. We, too, can grow stronger from our grief.

Carrying the Broken Tablets

The story of Moses ascending Mount Sinai to receive the Ten Commandments on two tablets is well known. What is less well known is that the first set of tablets God gave Moses was shattered. Moses threw them to the ground in a moment of despair. He returned to base camp and saw that the Israelites had resorted to their misguided ways and built a golden calf. What is most fascinating about this tale is that after receiving that second set of tablets, the shards from the first set weren't discarded. The Israelites carried the broken tablets, along with the whole ones, on their trek across the desert. They understood that life necessarily encompasses death, and living a wholehearted life requires us to carry broken fragments with us. Darkness is terrifying, but we have to be honest about it. That honesty is where we find the courage to confront and carry the unscathed tablets and broken pieces.

Being a spark seeker comes down to courage, though not in the usual sense of an act of bravery. Brené Brown, the author of *Daring Greatly: How the Courage to Be Vulnerable Transforms the Way We Live, Love, Parent, and Lead,* wrote, "Vulnerability is the birthplace of love, belonging, joy, courage, empathy, and creativity. It is the source of hope, empathy, accountability, and authenticity. If we want greater clarity in our purpose or deeper and more meaningful spiritual lives, vulnerability is the path."[57] She points out that the word *courage* comes from the Latin *cor,* which means "heart."

To live a life of courage is to live a life of heart—leading with one's heart, speaking from one's heart, and exposing one's heart.

Being courageous in this way doesn't mean we won't struggle. We will cower, tremble, and dance around the void at times, fearing the dark and its descent. We will have regrets, second-guess ourselves, stumble, and fall. To be spark seekers is to pick ourselves up, dust ourselves off, and keep seeking. We keep living, not in spite of our losses but because of them. We don't hide our broken hearts, but we carry them gently as part of the journey. As a result, we learn to live and love more wholly.

Susan Zimmerman in *Writing to Heal the Soul* shares the following:

> You have a story—a very important story that rests at the core of your being—to tell. It is a story that has torn your heart into pieces, and it is a story of beauty because your heart couldn't have been torn without first having loved and somehow lost something that you loved. Now is the time to begin honoring your story...blessed are the cracked for they shall let the light in.[58]

As a spark seeker, you tell the story of your life and that of your loved ones. Part of your story is bound in the process of seeking sparks in the dark. You fan those sparks into a flame and the flame into a fire. As you carry the qualities of your loved ones into the world, you live and love more fully and freely.

Our stories, bound up in a sea of memories, flow from person to person and generation to generation as we share our loves and losses. We reach the light by moving through the darkness and letting the light enter the cracks in our hearts. Our hearts can grow bigger, kinder, more compassionate, and more loving by bearing the pain of loss and learning its lessons. As spark seekers, we become light itself. We ignite the sparks of hope and healing. We shine that light as we live this one precious life and honor those we have loved.

I end this book with the words *l'chayim*—to life. Like the unexpected flower that grows between the cracks in the sidewalk, may we find the possible in what we thought was impossible, the hope within the sorrow, and the sparks within the dark. May we travel together from death's darkness into life's light, and may we be gentler and more loving with ourselves, and others, as a result. May we each move forward every day with courage and gentleness, compassion, and purpose. May we move forward as spark seekers, searching for meaning in our mournings and transforming death's darkness into life's light.

I invite you to continue your journey as a spark seeker at: www.sparkseekersthebook.com

ACKNOWLEDGMENTS

This book wouldn't be possible without the patience, love, and support of my beloved wife, Ariela. My love for her is a fire that grows stronger with each passing year; it warms my heart and brightens my life. Equally, this book wouldn't be possible without my beloved writing partner, Ellen Frankel. Ellen is the yin to my yang, keeps me on track, and has proven to be not only a writing partner but a soul sister. And thank you to her husband, Steve, who has been so generous with his time and who is our technology savior. To my children, Yehuda, Maya, Shoshana, and Aviv—everything I do is with the intention of bringing light into your lives, teaching you how to move through the dark and how to carry on as spark seekers long after I'm gone. To my mom, as the dedication states, your life illuminates my path and will continue to light the way for generations to come. To my sister, Rebecca Rosen, you have been a source of strength for me during times when I have wavered, given me a sense of certainty that there is, indeed, a life beyond where our beloved father now resides, and helped me integrate spirit into my life. To my brother, Zachary Perelman, stepfather Howard Goldstein, in-laws, aunts, uncles, and cousins—you're too many to name but part and parcel of my heart and my life. I love you all.

Thank you to all of my supporters and friends. To Jonathan and Rachelle Dubow and Tom and Amanda Clayman-Levenberg, I will always cherish our true and enduring friendship. To Rob and Stacy Edelstein, you have been continual friends and supporters. Thank you for this opportunity and privilege to work with you professionally, it is exciting and important work we are embarking upon. A special thank you to Karen and David Rosenberg; David, our brotherhood sustains me and your investment in me has made my work possible. In the spirit of Reb Nachman, you are, indeed, a warrior of light. To all of my friends from CSH and Boston's North Shore, you are too many to name but too important to go unmentioned. And to our new friends waiting for us in Eshchar, we are delighted to be a part of your community and already so grateful for all that you have done to make us feel at home. Thank you to all of my early readers whose suggestions have helped shape *Spark Seekers*: my father-in-law, Jim Kelch, Phyllis Karas, Mark Ankcorn, Lauren Weiss, my aunt Connie O'Connor, Marla Gay, Jerry Rosen, Doug Reeves, my uncle Dr. Larry Greenblatt, and Michele Tamaren – I so appreciate your time, feedback and encouragement. And a special thank you to Deb Laflamme for not only reading many versions of this book but also for passionately and effectively helping me share it with the world through your amazing company, FTLOYB—For The Love Of Your Biz and to Geralyn Miller of Geralyn Miller Design for translating my vision into a beautiful book cover design.

Thanks also to Paul Michaels and Man Mountain Productions, Inc.

ABOUT THE AUTHORS

Rabbi Baruch HaLevi

Baruch HaLevi, aka "Rabbi B," was ordained as a Conservative rabbi through the American Jewish University, Ziegler School of Rabbinic Studies, and received his doctoral degree in ministry from the Graduate Theological Foundation. For nearly a decade, Rabbi B, a motivational speaker and visionary, has served as spiritual leader of Congregation Shirat Hayam, a new synagogue created from the merger of two previous congregations. During his tenure, he helped transform this spiritual community into one of the most vibrant synagogues today, as exemplified in his book, also coauthored with Ellen Frankel, *Revolution of Jewish Spirit: How to Revive Ruakh in Your Spiritual Life, Transform Your Synagogue & Inspire Your Jewish Community* (Jewish Lights Publishing, 2012). In July 2015, Rabbi B and his family will be making aliyah, permanently moving to Israel, where he will be launching Rabbi B Initiatives, LLC, which will include Spark Seeker Ventures. This endeavor offers inspiring and innovative ways for spark seekers to mourn with meaning and to rethink ways of moving through dying and death to touch the fullness of life. You can learn more about Rabbi B and Rabbi B Initiatives through his blog, podcasts, and website at www.RabbiB.com.

Ellen Frankel

Ellen Frankel, LCSW is a grief counselor at Care Dimensions, a nonprofit hospice organization in Massachusetts. She's the author of *Beyond Measure: A Memoir about Short Stature and Inner Growth* (Pearlsong Press 2006) and the novel *Syd Arthur* (Pearlsong Press 2011). Ellen is also the coauthor of *The Diet Survivor's Handbook: 60 Lessons in Eating, Acceptance, and Self-Care* (Sourcebooks 2006); *Revolution of Jewish Spirit: How to Revive Your Spiritual Life, Transform Your Synagogue, & Inspire Your Jewish Community* (Jewish Lights Publishing 2012); and *The Comprehensive Guide to Treating Binge Eating Disorder, Compulsive Eating, and Emotional Overeating* (Routledge 2004, 2014 2nd ed.). You can visit Ellen at www.authorellenfrankel.com.

NOTES

1. Alan D. Wolfelt, PhD, CT, Companioning the Bereaved: A Soulful Guide for Caregivers, Kindle edition (Fort Collins: Companioning Press, 2006), 14.
2. Genesis 24:63
3. Rando, T. A. Treatment of Complicated Mourning. (Champaign, IL: Research Press 1993), 45.
4. Stephen King, The Shining (New York: Simon and Schuster, 2002), XVII
5. Wolfelt, Companioning the Bereaved, 14.
6. Timothy Williams, "Suicides Outpacing War Deaths for Troops," New York Times, June 8, 2012.
7. Tony Dokoupil, "Why Suicide Has Become an Epidemic—and What We Can Do to Help," Newsweek, May 23, 2013.
8. K. Schwartz, "Exploring family dynamics, eating attitudes and behaviors: A qualitative analysis of female children of Holocaust survivors," Dissertation Abstracts International: Section B: The Sciences and Engineering, no. 62 (2002): 4236.
9. Will Herberg, Judaism and Modern Man: An Interpretation of Jewish Religion (Woodstock, VT: Jewish Lights Publishing, 1951), 91.
10. Wolfelt, Companioning the Bereaved, 31.

11. Matt Sedensky, "Five Years after Schiavo, Few Make End-of-Life Plans," published March, 30, 2010, accessed November 14, 2014, http://www.nbcnews.com/id/36099208/ns/health-health_care/t/years-after-schiavo-few-make-end-of-life-plans/#.VGZqY4eN7d.

12. The Senior Outlook Today Team, "Americans Overwhelmingly Want Funeral Service, Still Few Preplanning," April 3, 2013, accessed November 14, 2014, http://www.senioroutlooktoday.com/americans-overwhelmingly-want-funeral-service-still-few-pre-planning/.

13. Marc Gafni, The Mystery of Love (New York: Simon & Schuster 2004).

14 "Discussions about Health: The Economics of the Funeral Industry," Homegoings, June 24, 2013, accessed on November 7, 2014, www.PBS.org.

15. Exodus 24:12

16. Brook Noel and Pamela D. Blair, I Wasn't Ready To Say Goodbye: surviving, coping & healing after the sudden death of a loved one (Naperville: Sourcebooks 2008) xxxii.

17. Interview with Alvin P. Sanoff, "One Must Not Forget," U.S. News & World Report, October 27, 1986, 68.

18. W. H. Frey II, D. D. Sota-Johnson, C. Hoffman, and J. T. McCall, "Effect of stimulus on the chemical composition of human tears," American Journal of Ophthalmology, no. 92 (1981): 559–567.

19. Peter McDonald, Sound Intentions: The Workings of Rhyme in Nineteenth-Century Poetry, eBook edition (New York: Oxford University Press, 2012), 246.

20. Elizabeth Kubler-Ross and David Kessler, On Grief and Grieving: Finding the Meaning of Grief through the Five Stages of Loss (New York: Scribner 2005), 756–768.

21. Psalm 30:5

22. David Eagleman, Sum: Forty Tales from the Afterlives, eBook version (New York: Knopf Doubleday Publishing Group, 2009), 23.

23. Psalm 121:5
24. Ernest Becker, The Denial of Death, eBook version (New York: Simon and Schuster, 2007), 11.
25. Matthew 27:46 (New International Version)
26. Luke 23:46 (New International Version).
27. Mother Teresa of Calcutta, Mother Teresa: Come Be My Light (New York: Doubleday Religious Publishing Group, 2009), 192.
28. Psalm 130:1
29. Kubler-Ross and Kessler, On Grief and Grieving Finding the Meaning of Grief Through the Five Stages of Loss, (New York, NY: Simon and Schuster 2007) 91.
30. Ernest Becker, Denial of Death, eBook version (New York, NY: Simon and Schuster, 2007), 16.
31. Psalm 23:4
32. Genesis 32:24–32
33. Quoted in Shelley Ramsey, Grief: A Mama's Unwanted Journey (WestBowPress, 2013), 13.
34. David Richo, The Power of Coincidence: How Life Shows Us What We Need to Know (Google eBook) (Boston: Shambhala Publications, 2007) 17.
35. Margery Williams, The Velveteen Rabbit, Or How Toys Became Real (New York: United Holdings Group, 1988), 7.
36. Ecclesiastes 23: 1–2, 4
37. Anthony Robbins, Giant Steps: Small Changes to Make a Big Difference (New York: Simon and Schuster, 2011), 71.
38. Rabbi Mark Gafni, "New Series of Blogs: Light From Darkness" accessed June, 28 2014, http://www.marcgafni.com/new-series-of-blogs-light-from-darkness-marc-gafni/.
39. Marianne Williamson, A Return to Love: Reflections on the Principles of a "Course in Miracles" (London: Thorsons, 1996), 190–191.
40. Viktor E. Frankl, Man's Search for Meaning (New York: Simon and Schuster, 1985), 86.

41. Brené Brown, The Gifts of Imperfection: Let Go of Who You Think You're Supposed to Be and Embrace Who You Are (Center City: Hazelden Publishing, 2013), 6.

42. Robert Moore and Douglas Gillette, "The Warrior and His Fullness," in The Awakened Warrior: Living with Courage, Compassion, and Discipline, ed. Rick Fields, A. Jeremy, and P. Tarcher (New York: Putnam Books, 1994), 29.

43. Ethics of Our Forefathers 2:16

44. Genesis 1:3

45. Henri Nouwen quoted in Sandy Fox, Creating a New Normal... After the Death of a Child, (Bloomington: iUniverse, 2010), 11.

46. Jerusalem Talmud, Sanhedrin 4:1 (22a)

47. Exodus 25:8

48. Quoted in Michael Terry editor, Reader's Guide to Judaism (New York: Routledge, 2013), 401.

49. Quoted in Archibald Henderson, George Bernard Shaw: His Life and Works (Whitefish, MT: Kessinger Publishing, LLC, 2004), 512.

50. Genesis 50:25

51. Genesis 40:4–5

52. Genesis 50:26

53. Rabbi Jonathan Sacks, The Chief Rabbi's Haggadah, (New York: Harper Collins, 2003), 29.

54. Exodus 13:19

55. Abraham Joshua Heschel, Who Is Man? (Redwood City: Stanford University Press, 1965), 99.

56. Accessed on May, 22 2014 http://www.imsdb.com/scripts/Road,-The.html, 103–104.

57. Brené Brown, Daring Greatly: How the Courage to Be Vulnerable Transforms the Way We Live, Love, Parent, and Lead (New York: Gotham, 2012), 27.

58. Susan Zimmerman, Writing to Heal the Soul (New York: Three Rivers, 2002), 28.

Made in the USA
Middletown, DE
29 April 2015